Jagadguru Maha Avatar Babaji

Sri Swami Vishwananda

UNITY WITH THE DIVINE

UNITY WITH THE DIVINE

By
Jagadguru Maha Avatar Babaji

Via
Utpalavati (Jean Peterson)

Scribe for *Unity with The Divine*

Disciple of Jagadguru Maha Avatar Babaji
&
Satguru Sri Swami Vishwananda

Babaji's dictation began August 18, 2008

Second Edition
Unity With The Divine

Notes To Readers

Maha Avatar Babaji informs us that he was present with each person who read the first edition. He communicated that he noticed some places within his text where his readers were perplexed.

In this second edition, for your benefit, Babaji has addressed concerns of the first edition readers by inserting illumination in certain places. As was truth for his first edition readers, Maha Avatar reminds us that he works with everyone through individual consciousness as each person chooses to attune to his vibration.

I also will be present with each of you who read this second edition. May you fulfill your heart's desire to experience the Divine facets of creation through conscientiously following life experiences, one by one, to the fullness of completion—Unity With The Divine.

—Babaji

CONTENTS

Contents continued Next Page

Contents continued....

ACKNOWLEDGMENTS

TO EVERYONE
Who contributed to the realization of Jagadguru Maha Avatar
Babaji's *Unity With The Divine*
We are grateful
THANK YOU

We thank Sri Swami Vishwananda for his loving and gracious
contribution of *The Transmission of Love Meditation* &
His message of Love in *Epistle Seventeen.*

We thank Swami Vishwavijayananda for
His courteous and gracious contribution of the photograph ©
Of His painting of Jagadguru Maha Avatar Babaji
on the Front and Back Cover

We thank Kena Peterson for the Contribution
Of Cover Design and Formatting.

We thank J. Marilyn Wilkinson, Ph.D
For lovingly contributing her expertise in the final edit.

FOREWORD

By Utpalavati *(Jean Peterson)*
Disciple Of
Jagadguru Maha Avatar Babaji
&
Satguru Sri Swami Vishwananda

Scribe for *Unity With The Divine*

Throughout human history the eternally snow-capped peaks of India's sacred Himalayan Mountains traditionally have been known as the home of the Immortal Gods. For millennia those high mountain regions of the Himalayas have been the sphere of the eternal, youthful form and spirit of the Physical-Light-Being mankind identifies as the Immortal Jagadguru Maha Avatar Babaji. For centuries, and perhaps millennia, many have encountered Babaji and subsequently identified him by various names. The names most attributed to him in present-day are Jagadguru Maha Avatar Babaji and the Immortal teacher; Maha means great and Avatar means the decent of divinity into physical form—Maha Avatar. Babaji means revered father and Immortal means one who lives forever. Hence: World Teacher, Immortal Jagadguru Maha Avatar Babaji. He informs us in these Epistles: "The various names attributed to me developed from certain divinely selected humans who came into contact with what appears to be my physical form roaming the mountain crags of the Himalayas in India and the vicinity of those high mountain regions."

Babaji may appear human at will and is reported to take many forms that have the ability to be in one or more places simultaneously. Maha Avatar is an Immortal Universal Being and he does not exclusively adhere to any singular tradition, religion, country, race or creed. He embraces with great unconditional love all spiritual traditions, all of creation and all consciousness as One. All the forms of Babaji come and go at will. Many people throughout the ages have interacted with him in the etheric, in seemingly physical form and in dreams, visions and meditations. The various forms of Babaji exemplify divine attributes and he invariably bestows many blessings and teachings upon those whom he encounters.

Babaji writes in *Epistle Six*: "Many synonyms for life exist in all Earth languages. For instance from ancient times in Hinduism there have been thousands of stories of the Gods with many faces and names. Ganesha, the elephant-faced God has been given many attributes; humans pray to obtain those same characteristics in their own lives. It is believed that Ganesha is the remover of obstacles. In resonance with that understanding psychological components of human anatomy allow the individual to attune his awareness to the attributes of Ganesha and then during prayer, meditation or puja worship, he may align with the Divine Principle exemplified in Ganesha and indeed obstacles in one's life may be transmuted. In a similar development to Ganesha, throughout the centuries, man has given me many names.

"I serve the Divine in the capacity of Good Will Ambassador to the world populations throughout the cycle of time in which you presently are living, the Kali Yuga, time of ignorance or darkness (completing and simultaneously merging into the next age known as the Golden Age, the Sathya Age—age of truth). *Throughout the centuries I have revealed myself to the few whom I choose to carry my message of Living Light of Love to those of mankind whom I am working with throughout their cycles of incarnations on Earth."*

Traditionally Babaji's mission includes assisting humanity to evolve at its own soul velocity into realization of its divine Oneness with God. The resulting Universal Love Vibration will transform and return this world and its living beings into the original Divine blueprint of paradise on Earth, the long prophesied Golden Era. It is said that whenever anyone speaks with reverence the name of Babaji, that person is given an instant spiritual blessing. Babaji offers humanity a glimpse of Divinity in physical form. He provides a conscious example of mankind's own possibilities for transforming himself from maya (illusion) into the Divine Immortal that Babaji has exemplified down through the centuries—an eternal bridge between The Divine and humankind.

Babaji's Purpose In Writing His Epistles

I awoke in bliss one morning in August 2008. Feeling a compelling impetus to meditate, I soon beheld Maha Avatar Babaji in His Immortal Form but seemingly physical. He moved toward me as if gliding along gracefully on a pathway of light. He came through energetic golden doorways, one after another, until He stood directly in front of me just inches from my eyes. As I looked into His beautiful Divine face and unfathomable eyes, I instantly became aware of myself in two dimensions simultaneously. While fully conscious of myself sitting in meditation, I simultaneously became aware of standing, pranaming, in front of Babaji in the Himalayas in India. Babaji sat on a low rock wall outside a familiar ashram built into a mountainside. To his right, rock steps led down the hillside to the fast-flowing Ganges River rushing along the valley floor on its way to eventually merge with the greater ocean. The crisp mountain air, stirred by a slight wind, gently blew Babaji's copper highlighted hair as his beautiful, celestial face smiled in greeting.

Babaji is very familiar to me as I remembered in 1985 of this lifetime that I have known him for "time out of mind." I am ecstatically happy to be in his Divine presence this crisp fall morning. Maha Avatar Babaji gracefully removes a sheet of parchment paper from an ivory cloth pouch casually slung across his chest. Babaji says: "I have written a series of *Epistles*. I request that you sit in meditation at 4:00 A.M. and begin recording as I deliver them to you. I will convey the *Epistles* to you over a short period of time in a divine heart to heart and mind to mind imprinting technique with which you are very familiar. Will you publish a "little book" containing the *Epistles*? I need only a "little book" to convey the steps to enlightenment into the consciousness of today's people around the world." I was astonished greatly that Babaji seemed to be paraphrasing John, disciple of Christ Jesus, who was told *not* to write the "little book" he was given as was recorded in the Christian *Bible* in the book of *Revelation.* Babaji informed the venerated Indian sage Lahiri Mahasaya in the latter nineteenth century: *When one feels unity with mankind all minds become transmitting stations that one can work with at will.*

Maha Avatar instructed me at the very beginning of his dictation: "The Guru-disciple relationship, by its very nature, exemplifies the mantra of duty for those who have attained a certain level of spiritual awareness. Sharing with humility one's spiritual experiences serves as inspiration and fortification for those who have gleaned spiritual strength and advancement from their own spiritual endeavors. In that way the Guru-disciple relationship matures through the millennia as spiritual aspirants walk the eternal way to enlightenment and unity with the Divine."

The task of bringing Babaji's book, *Unity With The Divine,* into physical manifestation has been a sacred trust of great joy, and his Divine blessing. I am eternally grateful for the experience and the opportunity to serve Beloved Babaji and you, his readers. May you attain unfathomable love and spiritual advancement in your future meditations through attuning to Babaji's vibration. I pray that you, who are guided from within, choose to accept Maha Avatar's Divine, loving invitation in *Epistle Six.* Seek out Sri Swami Vishwananda's *Atma Kriya* teachings that Babaji has entrusted him to place into present-day world consciousness. And may you, thereby, find that eternal peace and Divine Love are your daily companions.

PREFACE

By George
A Disciple of Sri Swami Vishwananda

Presented with the honorable task of writing this Preface to Maha Avatar Babaji's Epistles, I contemplated: "How does one write a Preface to the Word of a Divine Being?" I concluded that such a document only may be written with much humility, great reverence and gratitude.

Who is Babaji? First of all, Babaji is not a name but an appellation that means "Revered Father." In reading His Epistles you will see that Babaji tells us that He has been called many names by mankind throughout human history. Although the Maha Avatar often is identified with India and Hinduism and appears in the Himalayas in physical forms and many of His devotees are Indian, He certainly is not of one nation or one religion. Babaji is a Divine universal Being, like an Elder Brother in humanity's evolutionary development along its path to perfection. Three main attributes constitute His greatness—immense love, astonishing humility and unfathomable depth. He has a deep understanding of human nature in its plight to cope with the problems of survival and wellbeing in this world. His teachings always have been marked by a down-to-earth practicality, a hands-on attitude very rarely found in saints, a strange mix of purity, humility, love and pragmatism.

Some will not want to know what Maha Avatar Babaji reveals in His Epistles. Many people may find all this rather childish or naïve. If so, these Epistles are not for them as they will benefit more from spending their valuable time in the pursuit of life's plethora of the twenty-first century's enticing distractions.

Why does The Divine take the trouble to speak to mere mortals? Of course, He communicates out of Love—Divine Love—because He is our Friend. The expression "mere mortal" from His point of view is an illusion. He knows us from time immemorial as He has gifted us with His Breath of Life. This life is not the mortal life we identify as individual life (as we think), but rather it is the Eternal Breath of Life. *To The Divine we all are most valuable beings.* The Divine, existing eternally Omniscient (all knowing), Omnipotent (all powerful) and Omnipresent (existing everywhere as The One), may do all things simultaneously. Why then would not The Divine speak to the dear unenlightened humans, or more succinctly, to those souls who think that they are "just humans." After all, He has plenty of time!

The Divine speaks to humans in many voices and most of them are not vocal. He communicates with humans in every imaginable way and then some! It is a pity that we have such great difficulty in realizing this and in picking up His messages. Does the Divine get frustrated by this inability? Humans get frustrated, The Divine just smiles with love and metaphorically "laughs under his mustache," if He has one. You might ask: "Why does The Divine not speak more clearly if He knows that humans have a blockage in understanding what He is telling them?" My theory is that He knows that humans *eventually* will develop and grow spiritually to a point where they will understand and implement His messages; He wants them to achieve this *on their own.* Only then is it lasting and has value. The Divine does not use force in guiding humanity, although He very well could! This is the essence of wisdom.

At present the real problem is not that humans do not understand Him; it is rather that the vast majority *do not want to understand!* Humanity, as a whole, is seduced in our times by the modern distractions. This human condition is due to humanity getting carried away with the various ways of Earth life: mammoth egos out of control; the struggle for survival; the lust for power, money and sex; human fears and insecurities; yearning for the comfortable life and the quest for one's own elusive happiness quota. In these cases, say most people, "a bird in the hand is more valuable than two in the bush and there may not be any birds in the bush!"

Often humans listen to "The Voice of God" as conveyed to them by various clerics of all possible faiths. Generally speaking, most people are not inspired for they often perceive the flaws or the self-serving aspects of the so-called words of teaching and thereby become cynical. Because of that, to many, "religion" becomes a bad word. Many doubt the existence of The Divine. In today's world it is extremely difficult to detach from all this illusion and to become pure enough to hear The Voice. Maha Avatar Babaji's Epistles are presented in crystal clear words of higher teachings with such tangible Divine Love that the potential is there for those "who have ears to hear," to clear the debris from the pathway to the spiritual heart. And many of you will find yourselves embracing Maha Avatar's teachings in a familiar feeling and understanding: "I have known these words of truth and this Divine Love somewhere before! Is it part of my nature or part of my memory?"

Sometimes The Divine decides to express His messages in a more explicit form, for instance in black and white—a language most people can understand. He has been doing this for centuries, even for millennia, and The Word is thereby recorded in humanity's' Holy Books. The writings were revealed or inspired by Teachers, Masters, Prophets, historical figures, both mythical and unknown authors and anonymous poets or visionaries. The timely messages frequently were for a certain age and most often were written for certain people in each time period. Some of these books are very well known and have become universal Bibles, some are more obscure or addressed to specialized groups, and some have been lost in the sands of time. Still the messages have flowed to humanity throughout the ages and continue to be received in present time and perhaps even more prevalently today, I suspect.

One thing we are beginning to realize in our age: *"There is no single message."* as most religions preach. Humanity develops and changes as the ages change. We are not necessarily more spiritual today than say, 5,000 years ago. Probably at that time there were a higher proportion of more highly spiritually developed humans. It was easier then; there were fewer distractions, temptations, less clutter, fewer vibrations and definitely less noise. People and their lives were simpler and concentration was easier. Yet, we have become much more complicated beings today and live in an environment which is complex, demanding and continuously changing. A major acceleration has taken place. Things happen much faster and change much faster. Within one lifetime a human experiences things both novel to the past and also equal to many lives of the past. We are bombarded by information, messages, temptations and many newly identified vibrational frequencies. One may conclude that humanity is simultaneously going through a magnificent and great test while walking through the threshold of a grand evolutionary change.

In the midst of all this, and while living in the twenty-first century's collective consciousness of exploding sensations, Utpalavati (the scribe of Babaji's Epistles, Jean Peterson), with her acute spiritual sensitivity receives Maha Avatar Babaji's message clearly and lucidly. Paralleling Lord Shiva's, *Shiva Sutras,* Babaji's Epistles necessitate no commentary. And Babaji conveys His message with immense love and great clarity. For those of us who want to listen to Maha Avatar's message, His Epistles speak loud and clear. I do not think all will listen to Maha Avatar Babaji's words, or that they will change to the extent He says is relevant and possible for them, except for the few. In Christianity, Christ Jesus tells a parable about the shepherd who leaves his flock of 100 sheep to save one lamb. Jesus teaches that maximum effort is a worthy cause to save even one soul. Jesus also says that not all the seed falls on fertile soil; some is wasted, some washed away, and some does not take solid root. All soil is not equally receptive but a tiny seed eventually grows into a magnificent tree.

Babaji has taught repeatedly that one perfected human being is like a crystal. Scientific knowledge demonstrates that a crystal placed in a certain liquid solution attracts and creates more crystals in an ever-expanding agglomeration of crystals which form around the original one crystal. The original crystal is symbolically the catalyst and the solution is the world that spawns more crystals or more perfected human beings. According to Babaji one perfected human has a disproportionate influence over those around him, just by his existence. I think *that* is what Babaji is offering with His

Epistles—the chance for the few human beings, who become committed and continue to connect with him in meditation, the opportunity with His blessing, to change into a perfected or enlightened Jivan Mukta (enlightened while in body). Then those few may potentially and exponentially change the world collective consciousness into the unification of purity.

Babaji tells us that the right kind of meditation is like "churning the ocean of milk" in the Indian story in which the objective is to create out of the milk, butter, and out of the butter the ambrosia of immortality. To a rational being, it must be worthwhile to make the maximum effort to gain the elixir of immortality, the dream of humanity through the ages. I pray that the "few" who read these Epistles and apply what is taught by Maha Avatar Babaji will benefit more than they can now imagine. Even more, I pray that this serious effort of those few committed ones will greatly enhance humanity's chances of surviving these last days of the Kali Yuga as Earth and humanity merge together into the Golden Era just over the horizon.

EPISTLE ONE

Greetings,

I am the one whom humanity identifies as Jagatguru Maha Avatar Babaji. I come to you all riding the cosmic blue ray of freedom, speaking to you from the heart of all mankind.

Mathematical numbers, squared, as in $4^2 = 16$ [4 x 4]; $16^2 = 256$ [16 x 16] assist in providing an understanding that everything squared takes creation into the point of equality and freedom. The story of the City Four Square as written by the disciple of Christ, John, in the Christian Bible's King James Version, is in the book of *Revelation*. The City Four Square, as terminology, is divine symbolic language that provides a picture of creation's mathematical formula for the present Kali Yuga age (age of darkness, iron age) to flow into new birth of Sathya Yuga (age of truth) through freedom's gate of Self-realization, union with The Divine. The gateway into the City Four Square is available to each and every one of you; it lies within, safely sealed inside a crystalline matrix of subatomic knowledge that you all possess.

The mathematical genius of one gifted with the brilliance of the scientist, Albert Einstein, takes the world intellect into a new dimension of understanding. ($E = mc^2$ — the connection Einstein discovered between energy and mass is expressed in the equation, $E = mc^2$. Therein, E = energy, m = mass, and c^2 represents the very large number— the square of the speed of light).

A new dimension of being is what we hope to accomplish in the *Epistles* in *Unity With The Divine*. We wish mankind to stop consuming present-day identification of the real world as the scenario he finds around him and, instead, focus inside the self, the real self, the real world. It is time in man's historical record of time for him to follow the call from the crystalline matrix in the deepest, innermost self that is the true reliance, trust and truth that God lovingly has provided him. Wake yourselves up to truth and be free.

Let us begin with a small dissertation on the circle of time. As a soul evolves in lifetime after lifetime on Earth, he is born into bodies that offer the greatest opportunity to evolve into the next level of mathematical equation for human attainment. Souls ensnared upon the wheel of karma must begin, at some point, to free themselves from the spokes of the wheel and go within to the center. It is in the center of the wheel where one finds the real Self. And therein one finds peace, equality with all of creation, love, harmony and the stillness where God resides.

Krishna came some five thousand years ago to planet Earth and showed mankind, by his life lived in perfect conentment and the grace of love divine, how to live each day to the fullest of its capacity. He did not waste a minute of that life. Krishna was aligned continuously with the inner self and his mission or reason for being on the planet at that time. Read the *Bhagavad Gita* and comprehend the vastness of God's Will for His Creation; read of the potentiality of mankind as a soul who lives forever and ever. As the mind and the heart of man grasps that great truth, he will be well on the way to finding the real world that lies within the heart and soul like a seed crystal of pure love and understanding.

I beseech you, my Earth brethren of present time, to search also within the mathematical formula the Christ has given you in the crucifixion story of the birth, transformation and transfiguration. You live forever! Your consciousness cannot be extinguished as it is God Himself residing inside you. *We are all one!* It is from that great understanding and atmic (soul) comprehension that we will walk Christ's path of birth, transformation and transfiguration into new birth with the *Eighteen Epistles* we humbly offer you with Love in *Unity With The Divine.* Let us prepare ourselves in thought, word and deed each day to align ourselves with the Divine Will for our lives that we know resides within our very own atmic soul.

Be free to explore within you the vast Ocean of Milk* where the Sea of Vishnu takes you when you are brave enough to step into the lifeboat Vishnu provides for each and every one of you. Lord Vishnu is the sustainer-preserver of the Universal mathematical formula that sustains the life-force of man. Vishnu will guide you and navigate your boat of life safely into Shiva's** Ocean of Milk which lies in equality within each man, woman and child on planet Earth.

Receive the blanket of love the Gods wish to wrap around you and let it take you home to the everlasting peace you all long to remember, live and rest within.

—*Babaji*

(*—**) See Glossary

EPISTLE TWO

Beloved Friends,

The following meditation experience of Utpalavati especially was designed for my disciple, who is serving as my scribe for these *Epistles*. I have chosen it as the introduction to *Epistle Two* as edification for both the readers and those of you who choose to meditate with me in your future. The meditation offers a concise, coherent example of what is possible on the spiritual path as I work throughout the long millennia with my disciples.   *—Babaji*

Utpalavati's Meditation:

I am consciously aware of myself in two dimensions as I sit in meditation. I am completely aware in my home in America and simultaneously in the great sacred India with Maha Avatar Babaji. Beckoning me to follow, he says: "Come, sit with me on the banks of the Ganges". He leads me to sit under a certain banyan tree in Serampore, India that I immediately recognize. It is the great banyan tree standing where the ashram and ancestral home of Swami Sri Yukteswar Giri, Paramahamsa Yogananda's Guru was located. I visited there when I was with Sri Swami Vishwananda's free Medical Camp in Kolkata, India in December 2007. In present-day, the temple and shrine of Yukteswar is on the same grounds where his ashram used to be located, and his vibration is beautifully and divinely powerful in and around the grounds of the temple. The banyan tree Maha Avatar and I are sitting under is the same one where Babaji appeared to Sri Yukteswar when he had completed the book Babaji had requested that he write, *The Holy Science.*

As I sat under the great banyan tree on the banks of the Ganges with Babaji, for a few minutes I gazed into India's most sacred river. I thought of the pollution in the Ganges and in the world presently. I wondered if it was as prevalent in Sri Yukteswar's day. Then I calmed my mind through a certain knowing within that

Babaji wished it. Suddenly I remembered the story of Babaji's meeting with Sri Yukteswar under this same banyan tree nearby to his ancestral home and ashram in Serampore, India.

Sri Yukteswar was in Allahabad, India at the Kumbha Mela (spiritual gathering of several thousand) held in January 1894 at the encouragement of his guru, the great Lahiri Mahasaya.

There he met a *saint*, Maha Avatar Babaji. The saint initiated Sri Yukteswar as a Swami and requested he write a book. Babaji instructed Yukteswar to write a comparison of the basic unity between the teachings of Christ Jesus in Christianity and the Hindu scriptures such as *The Bhagavad Gita*. Maha Avatar *promised* that he would meet Yukteswar again after the book was completed.

After Yukteswar's *The Holy Science* was finished Babaji, as he had promised appeared to Yukteswar under the banyan tree on the banks of the Ganges in Serampore, India at Yukteswar's ashram. When Yukteswar returned from obtaining sweets, Babaji and the group of disciples who were with him had disappeared. Later when Yukteswar saw Babaji make an appearance at the home of Lahiri Mahasaya, Babaji laughingly told him that the energy of Sri Yukteswar's excitement and restlessness had literally propelled Babaji and his disciples back into the ethers.

It was the fulfillment of Babaji's promise to meet Sri Yukteswar when his book was completed that brought him to meet Yukteswar under the same banyan tree that I would meet Babaji, in etheric form, in September of 2008 and 104 years later in this meditation. Paralleling Yukteswar's meeting with Babaji in Allahabad, he spoke to me further about producing this book of his *Epistles*.

I realize that it is *immensely easier* to quiet the mind while in etheric form rather than the physical, and I silently and gratefully thanked Sri Yukteswar for revealing his (physical) experience with Babaji. I knew it was the remembrance of Sri Yukteswar's story that allowed me to quiet my mind, thereby stabilizing the energetic connection between Babaji and myself.

Sitting with Maha Avatar Babaji on the banks of the Ganges in wondrous etheric form, my now quieted mind and eyes were magnetically and peacefully directed to the beautiful, celestial form of Babaji sitting on my left. Babaji gracefully and lovingly turned to face me and gently placed five white pieces of candy on my palm. They were round candy sticks about five inches in length. Babaji said: "Please give one of these candies to: (He named five people). From time to time when I appear to my devotees, I give them sweets. I request that you [Utpalavati] deliver these etheric candy sticks to those devotees I have designated. At that time, I understood that Babaji wished me to write the five people to deliver His message and etheric candy to them. All five had developed the ability to understand such a gift as well as Babaji's delivery method. Therefore, Babaji left it to the free will of the five individuals to accept His blessing and gifts or not. *Likewise,* Maha Avatar is now offering his book of *Epistles* and readers freely may choose to accept his gift and blessings or not!

Maha Avatar concluded my private time with him while smiling radiantly and saying: "My love for you all is eternal." He then began the following *Epistle Two.*

Babaji: The following *Epistle* is addressed to the disciples of Sri Swami Vishwananda; I am his guru. This *Epistle* serves as introduction to those of you who feel you do not know me or do not, as yet, remember me. Please read this *Epistle* standing true to your Divine Heart nature, and you will comprehend fully what I am writing indirectly to each of you "between the lines."

It is time that people who are connected in the physical through their Spiritual Teacher, Sri Swami Vishwananda, begin to take seriously their commitment to their Teacher and their commitment to their own advancement into light. I request that those of you to whom I am speaking, lay aside any differences or doubts you may have and attune yourselves with the teachings of your Guru, your teacher and your path of Bhakti Marga, the spiritual path of love and devotion. It is that kind of commitment for which we are searching to locate in Swami Vishwananda's devotees and disciples.

I am coming to you in this way, via heart to heart and mind to mind communication so that we may encourage and inspire you on your path in yet another way. I wish to inspire you to go inside and find a place of firm commitment that not even an earthquake can shake. I wish you to feel free to call on me and your Guru or your spiritual teacher to help you find that place inside yourself. I communicate to you, this day, that all of you have a good chance to move yourselves into the dimension of enlightenment should you choose to focus on your advancement into spiritual freedom rather than the chaos men's minds are creating at present time in the world of illusion.

Let us please stand firm on this: I am requesting an internal commitment from each of you. Will you meditate with me and commit sincerely to your own enlightenment and to Sri Swami Vishwananda and your spiritual path? *This communication in no way negates your true internal connection to The Divine.* This way of reaching you is truly in juxtaposition with your own avenues of connection and attunement with the Divine; that is all!

Pray, my friends, for the safe journey of Bhakti Marga which is the path of love and devotion in whatever your spiritual tradition may be, to travel safely into the New Age on your horizon. Pray for the All of creation to come home to the holy light of the manna The Divine wishes to shower upon you all should you be willing to receive it. Pray that your world recovers from the pollution man has fostered upon his home, Mother Earth. Determine fully, completely, vertically and horizontally* that you will be a part of the solution and not part of the problem to your Guru, your Spiritual Teacher, as he strives to bring his committed disciples into alignment with Divine Will.

My message to you all this day for both *all readers* and the disciples and devotes of Sri Swami Vishwananda is this: I am encouraging you to choose rightly (dharmically) by focusing *less* on the world of illusion and thereby committing whole-heartedly to your Spiritual Teacher, whomever it may be, and your spiritual path in Divine Love, Patience and Unity.

My Love for you all is eternal.

—Babaji

*Note: Babaji is speaking about the symbology of the **divine energetic cross; [+]—Vertical**—connection to The Divine; and **horizontally**—connection to the material Earth and physical body.

EPISTLE THREE

To Those Whom I write,

From the dawn of time most of mankind has believed that the higher dimensions of the cosmos were beyond their reach and experience. In order for humanity to form a pathway to the higher dimensions, The Divine continuously has been sending enlightened teachers to man-kind throughout time. Through the teachings of the enlightened beings, religions have sprung up into the matrix of human endeavors. In their beginning each religion that has withstood the passage of time and events on Earth was initiated by an enlightened Master who was given a dispensation from the Father, The One. The Master then created a formula for enlightenment within his teachings. All religions in their purest form are based, by this means, on the same Divine Principle of God, The Father-Mother. Divine Love, as taught by these Masters, leads each person to go within into matrix of his own divinity.

As time meanders into infinity on Earth after the Masters who created the religions have left the physical body and the material world, the religions they created became weakened or polluted as succeeding generations of mankind created dogmas around the original pure teachings of the Masters.

These *Epistles* direct you to go *within* where all knowledge is stored through using meditation as your pathway. *We are not judging any religion* when we inform you that we want to lead you to go within your inner self in meditation and there you will find your own pure sathya, truth. In so doing, you will unearth the Universe, the whole Cosmos that lies within you.

Let us understand from the beginning of these *Epistles*, that we are one in body, one in heart and one in soul, or three-in-one, the Trinity. From that premise we will remember that the number

$3^2 = 9$. Nine is a holy number of spirituality standing as a sentinel for completion into the whole, oneness. The number nine translated into itself, such as $9 + 9 = 18$ and $1 + 8 = 9$; and $18 + 18 = 36$ and $3 + 6 = 9$. Always nine translated into itself equals nine, the whole or oneness into infinity. *Nine is the number that created your universe.*

In the past the Sri Yantra was only comprehended and drawn by the Vedic masters and scholars. In present day, it quite easily and commonly is understood that it is simply nine triangles intersected. Your Universe is also constructed from the mathematical number nine and the sacred geometry of the Sri Yantra. Let us remember that, as we are one, we stand in the eternal light of The Father of us all. Christ said: 'My Father and I are one." And so it is for all of creation.

Jesus Christ knew the mathematical formula for wholeness, completion—the number nine. His life was a demonstration of how to take the human body and translate it into the finer energy of The Divine. The crucifixion story outlines the mathematical formula of transfiguration into light body. Do you, now in the twenty-first century, attune to Christ's vibration in a way that will lead you through "the valley of the
shadow of death" into the oneness of the cosmos? Let it be so! Attune to the Enlightened Master on your planet whom you choose from the heart; *surrender to his teachings* and permit him to lead you into your own enlightenment.

In this age, the Kali Yuga is ascending from its long, dark descent and is now rising into the New Age of Golden Light, We encourage you to hold the hand of an Enlightened Master, your spiritual teacher of any tradition or your Satguru, and take the steps necessary to evolve yourselves into the realms of higher consciousness. We aim to lay out the steps to enlightenment, one by one, in *Unity With The Divine.* I say to those of you reading these *Epistles,* "Take the hand of your teacher, your guru, your Satguru; *take my hand* and let us walk together into light, the life-force of The Divine. Inside all of you exists the seed crystals of Prema, [love], Sathya [truth], Dharma [right action], Shanti [peace], Unity [oneness] and Ahimsa [non-violence]. Let yourselves be aware of all these in every thought, word and deed. And you will be free.

My friends choose to lighten the load of all your brothers and sisters by lightening your own load of darkness. Be free of the seven deadly sins, so identified: Lust, gluttony, greed, sloth, jealousy, wrath, envy, pride. They are indeed heavy burdens to bear. Lay them at the feet of your Guru, your spiritual teacher. Delete these from your consciousness and transform into light. Let us attune ourselves each day to the Divine Principles of Prema, Sathya, Dharma, Shanti, Unity and Ahimsa. The first five, once attained, will naturally transport you into Ahimsa (non-violence and peace). Shanti, peace, will reign on this planet when every man, woman and child lives these Divine Principles. You then will be in the Golden New Age that beautifully exists just over the horizon of mankind's darkest hours that now hang like a thick but still semi-translucent haze over your planetary matrix.

We are indeed one with the Universal Consciousness. Be a part of the *solution* to Earth's problems instead of part of the *problem*. To the degree that you are committed to living the mathematical formula that we have outlined, through solving life's problems as they apply to your situation in life, so let it be.

—*Babaji,* One aspiring in these *Epistles* to be your guide into
   Mankind's New Age of Freedom.

EPISTLE FOUR

Dearest Friends,

Rest assured that a Divine timing for restoration follows the destruction that is necessary for any reformation to bring forth the light of day. When you attune to the Christ light within, you see the crystal clear view of the times ahead when the world will bow to light. Today in your time the flow of events in the arena of time is allowing you to feel the turmoil within each individual as the Christ light waits in patient silence for each man, woman and child on your planet to come into his own knowing from within.

The winds of change blowing upon the face and heart of each person incarnated has been whipping into a whirlwind since the 1960s in your time. When people came to me in the Himalayas in those early years of the 1970s I came into the world of form in several bodies to assist in lighting the way of the wayfaring pilgrim. *So it is today in the early years of the twenty-first century, I am available to you in several forms on the planet.* You who wish to transform into the New Age vibration of light must search me out if you wish to see and connect with me in form. You will know me and learn to recognize me from within your spiritual heart.

In former times of great transformation you may observe from history that great wars ushered in the light amongst the darkness of hate, greed and all the turmoil of war. It is in the restoration that must follow war wherein the true character of mankind comes from deep within to rebuild both the material destruction and the emotions and heart of man. Therefore if man chooses war then the Divine provides an opportunity for light to come from the darkness of war through the restoration that must follow. The hearts of man in this time try to tune out war happening in other parts of the world. Your leader's then take command of the situation of your inattention or lack of taking responsibility for decisions and actions your leaders choose. And that pulls countries into the headstrong leadership that brings about the bullies of the world: the dictators, the presidents, the czars, the premiers.

Let us for a moment think about the ramifications of war. Look at World War II. That was a time in the history of man when the world could know shortly after an event what had transpired across the oceans of your world. And so for the first time in written history mankind could begin to think of himself as the possibility of one family being present upon the planet. And that comprehension in present-day brings light even as the destruction of war rages on. Today technology has advanced so rapidly since the 1930s and 1940s that you may watch and hear the war zone in the same instant it is happening. You must pay attention to what is occurring across your planet, your home.

My friends, it is time to begin to harmonize your own life with the tenets of old. Relearn from within your being how to survive the turmoils of your world. *Meditate each day*. Transformation and peace must come from within your essence. Overwhelming issues exist with the planet's evolution at this time. Pollution, political turmoil, environmental and social issues need to come into alignment with light. This can only occur when each one of you goes within and aligns yourself with light. Can you remove darkness? Can you command it to move away from you? Can you legislate or govern in a way that darkness no longer exists? No! You cannot. What to do then? You must bring light into the realm of darkness wherever light is needed. With emancipation, your world and your citizens may live in love, in peace and in harmony with nature, with each other and with the sky of tomorrow lit with the transformation of hearts burning with passion for the divine light of freedom. Harmony comes from within when one is alighted with everlasting love which is divine.

Each of you is following a path in your present incarnation. Each of you is aligning with light or with the darkness of misunderstanding of why you have incarnated at this time and into the circumstances you have been born into. I ask those of you who are reading these *Epistles* to align with light. What is this light of which I am speaking, do you think? *I ask you with inmost sincerity that you meet me in meditation and I will teach you what you need to know about light and dark. Many of you know that the time is ripe for the fruit of the vine to be plucked, the cosmic adventure to begin for you. I can help you.*

Now is the time of transformation upon your planet like it never has happened before. Due in part to the light that has been brought through instant communication you all know that your world is in crisis. Band together, those of you who know the signs of the times, and walk in light of knowing. Look in your lives and begin to arrange them as if the Christ, the Buddha, the Yogi, the Zen Master and all the Masters of the world's religions were breathing down your necks with the warning that your world's future existence, *Nay*, the very light of life, stands in danger of being extinguished should you as a nation, a continent and world family *not* come into alignment with light.

Come to me those of you who feel so moved to meet me in meditation. Come with the Christ light within all of you blazing for reformation. Then you will know your future is assured to belong to the future generations of mankind who will walk in the new age of freedom. In that day the lion will lay down with the lamb and the Christ Child will be born with each new babe. Then the society and the planetary population will exist in political freedom aligned with the One Light of the Masters of Light who have revealed to you the way to freedom.

Let us come together in mediation and you will find peace; you will find the love of the Christ within you. Let the signs of the times lead you to God, the One Light. Let your transformation begin from this day forward. If you were drowning and going down for the third time all that you would want is oxygen, to rise again to the surface and breathe the breath of life. *Want God like that!* Align all your systems within you with that wish, that command of your thoughts and knowing. Learn passionately to want the knowledge of light and love within you to guide your life with the intensified fervor a drowning person creates for the desire for one more breath that is so focused that it can save him from a drowning death.

In present time, turmoil reigns on your world. Let your focus be one-pointed and let God be your guide. He loves you one and all, therefore decide this day to let it be your focus to walk in light of understanding and love divine. I am Babaji, one who wishes for you to take freedom's reins into your hands and transform yourselves and your world into light. And fractionally, with each doing his part, it literally will save you and your world. Then the divine plan for Earth thereby will be transformed into wholeness of the One that surely will materialize before your eyes. If you close yourselves from within and focus only on the outer world, you see blindly, and darkness will reign. Bring light to your world and to your fellowman by meditation and going within where the light of understanding and the comprehension of God's laws will replace the old outworn laws of materialism. Come home to freedom, my friends, and let it be.

I love you all dearly.

—*Babaji*

EPISTLE FIVE

Beloved Friends Reaching for Cosmic Consciousness,

Nature dawned on Earth. And since that exact time, as you know it, nature began in all its sequential efforts to teach mankind the lessons of Divine Will. Nature has cycles from the rose in springtime bloom to winter's silence and then it returns to spring and, again, the blooming. *In time,* man began to play with the idea that his own will was paramount to the will of creation, forgetting that he is one with creation itself. And through it all, the ego developed into the monstrous will of human collective consciousness.

The strongest will among you on the planet in any given timeframe molds or influences greatly the will of each of you. Out of that consciousness level mass historical events are created and unfold into third dimensional dramatizations of illusion you call life. Understand that all events, from the sacrifice of Christ on the Cross to Hitler's drama starting in the county of Germany that spread like a virus into the whole world, have been created by all of you together in collective consciousness.

The strongest rule your world and, thereby, gather their followers who group together and impose their will on the world population. *Ones like Christ come from the light to help you perceive that you also are light.* You must go within the essence of yourself, however, to reveal the light and to allow it to shine and then darkness will disappear without a fight. Mahatma Gandhi was one who showed the way how to shine light into darkness to cause it to disappear without friction or resistance. Gandhi took the pathway of both inner and outer peaceful nonviolence, ahimsa.

You may read in your historical recordings of Nelson Mandela of South Africa who was imprisoned for twenty-seven years. But was he in prison really? Nelson Mandela showed you all that the physical form may be locked within a stone prison but the spirit, the essence of your eternal soul, your consciousness, is always free. He took the path of active resistance in the outer world but showed humankind the way to inner freedom.

I urge you all to create a pathway within yourselves to the freedom that South Africa's Nelson Mandela found within himself during the time of his physical imprisonment. And the pathway of India's Gandhi, when followed, will lead you to both inner and outer freedom. *Meditation is the key to the doorway that leads to freedom.* I have given *Atma Kriya* techniques to Sri Swami Vishwananda. The next *Epistle*, number six, will carry my message to you of how you may attune your vibration with mine through the divine teachings of *Atma Kriya* by Sri Swami Vishwananda. (Reference Appendix I for information about *Atma Kriya* and Swami Vishwananda.)

Today, with the current status of instant communication, collective mind is influenced with so many varying wills of the strongest among you that your psyche or conscious mind is overwhelmed with stimuli. You now have most people on the planet using mind-altering substances because they cannot be alone with their fears and thoughts even for a moment. This state of the world prompted one of your singers of a recent era to state when asked if he used the drug, heroin: "I'm for anything that gets you through the night."

And so the populous of the world at present sits on a precipice within the mind in fear of what man has created and he must live, in the waking state. And he fears even more the void or unknown that jumping off the cliff offers if he decides to explore his inner world, his essence, that place where the real self is revealed. It is that inner space I wish to assist you in searching out the courage to explore in these *Epistles* sent to you with most sincere Divine Love.

A small story:

The following small story will demonstrate for you how Divine Will creates freedom, harmony, peace and liberation, salvation, when one is in attunement. Together, let us walk through the following scenes from lifetimes that were exper-ienced by one of my disciples who has been with me through-out eternity. *His ribbons of time expressed as life experiences have the potential to lead you into your own ribbons of time or energetic pathways to freedom.* That freedom lies within you and you do not have to go anywhere to get it. You do not have to create a war to locate real freedom. You only need to meditate and your very own energetic pathway will open itself and reveal your path.

Come with me on a journey that for my readers will be imaginary, but that one of my disciples did indeed take on his self-chosen path back home. Once in a long ago time, deep in his cave nestled among the crags of the Indian Himalayas, a yogi sat in meditative bliss, or samadhi. I came and sat with him by the dancing bright orange and red flames of his dhuni (a sacred fire). The yogi, my disciple, instantly knew my presence had entered his vicinity and briefly opened his eyes to acknowledge that I sat there with him.

You may wonder how a yogi was able to instantly come back from samadhi to physical reality. A truly advanced yogi is aware of the totality of creation in every instant; indeed the yogi is omnipresent. You may have read of people trying to get the attention of yogis in the Himalayas who sit in samadhi, and they are unable to do so even when they make the choice to inflict physical harm upon the yogi's physical body.

Know that the advanced yogi is fully aware at all times of what is occurring to his physical form and indeed in all of creation. It is, therefore, the yogi's choice whether or not he entertains the persistent person's desire to get his attention! I know that those of you who are reading these *Epistles* want to attain that degree of Cosmic Consciousness! As I have said, you must want moksha, liberation, like a drowning man wants the oxygen of one more breath. You must create the intensity of desire for enlightenment like the drowning man also desires breathing in air to continue to be his lot in life.

At the time I sat in his cave and at his sacred fire with my disciple, he was a fully God-realized being. The Divine had requested that he return soon to the physical body as a yogi teacher at the level of higher consciousness. He was to teach the Divine sacred Vedic knowledge of Cosmic Consciousness *through example.* He was to be born into the ruling class in India in the city of Ayodhya, India. I was to watch over him in the projected lifetime and lead him step-by-step to his life's work. His future parents were highly evolved and enlightened Divine Beings.

My disciple had been spending most of his time in Samadhi since The Divine request had registered in his consciousness. One night, since I am his Guru, I came to sit with him in his Himalayan cave to meditate and speak with him about the Divine request. I asked my beloved disciple when he planned to return to the physical and if there were anything I could do to assist him? I reminded him of the Cosmic Law that states that an evolved soul who has mastered the Earth experience has a duty to help his still unenlightened brothers in the physical. Upon hearing counsel, my disciple soon embarked on a physical lifetime being born in the city of Ayodhya, India as a son of the ruling royal couple of that city. He was given the birth name, *Lava.*

Centuries later, Lava took birth into a present-day western country literally on the other side of the world from India in the east. Lava made some unwise choices in some of his lifetimes since his incarnation in Ayodhya that brought his vibration down from his former enlightened status. Still retaining some small degree of his former enlightened yogic powers, or siddhis, Lava was born with a burning desire to fulfill his spiritual destiny in the present lifetime and thereby attain liberation once again. Those ribbons of time bring Lava to his present life dilemma in 2009 of the twenty-first century.

Lava is one of my disciples who will become intimately acquainted with these *Epistles* and will take them to heart and practice. Lava will attain liberation once again in his current lifetime.

Know that I am on a search for many more of you presently living on Earth and who <u>now</u> are ready to reach for Cosmic Consciousness. <u>I know who you all are!</u>

I am Babaji of the majestic Himalayas, the sacred mountains of India that stand as eternal sentinels of Love, Devotion, Trust, and the everlasting Divine Will of Unity. My offer of assistance is eternally vigilant, even as the great Himalayan Mountains have stood throughout time as spiritual sentinels for mankind. I ask sincerely: Are you ready?

EPISTLE SIX

Dear Friends and Students,

Many synonyms for life exist in all Earth languages. For instance from ancient times in Hinduism there have been thousands of stories of the Gods with many faces and names. Ganesha, the elephant-faced God has been given many attributes; humans pray to obtain those same characteristics in their own lives. It is believed that Ganesha is the remover of obstacles. And so the psychological components of human anatomy allow the individual to attune his awareness to the attributes of Ganesha. During prayer, meditation or puja worship to Ganesha one may align with the Divine Principle embodied in the murti (statue) and indeed obstacles may be transmuted. This is a way for humanity to attune with Divine Love and walk into the Light of Life as the darkness of ignorance or separation from the Creative Force, Divine Principle, or God as an obstacle in the life is restored to wholeness.

In a similar development to Ganesha, throughout the centuries man has given me many names. I quietly have remained in the background of political, economic and social activities on Earth. Presently, man identifies me mainly with the names of Jagadguru Maha Avatar Babaji and the Immortal Babaji. Those names developed from certain divinely selected humans who came into contact with what appears to be my physical form roaming the mountain crags of the Himalayas in India, Tibet and in the vicinity of those high mountain regions. The combination of those two names simply means Revered Father who lives forever.

I serve the Divine in the capacity of Good Will Ambassador to the World populations. In the Himalayan culture of the Yogis your current age is identified as the Kali Yuga, time of ignorance or darkness. Throughout all the centuries I have revealed myself to the few who then carry my message of Living Light of Love to those of mankind with whom I am working throughout their incarnations on Earth. In Divine timing, each heart and mind that I have prepared throughout the centuries comes into awareness of me, and that I have lived on the planet for centuries and throughout all of their lifetimes on Earth. *Awareness of me comes when the Soul Light has matured the body consciousness into vibrational attunement with my Essence that mankind identifies as The Immortal Jagadguru Maha Avatar Babaji*

And so it is that you are reading these *Epistles* coming through the heart and mind of one among you whom I have prepared throughout the soul's incarnational cycles on Earth. You who are guided to read these *Epistles* are among the souls with whom I have worked to bring into Divine Enlightenment. These *Epistles* are designed to assist you into the freedom available in your time whereby you may walk in Living Enlightenment or the Jivan Mukta, freed while in body.

Forty Day Meditation Technique

For forty days consecutively, I invite you to rest awhile in quietness as I lead you in meditation to attune you to my vibration. Therein only Divine Light registers upon any third dimensional instrument that presently has the capacity to identify vibration or movement of light upon the sound and material waves which comprise the elements of matter or form.

My invitation requests that you meditate <u>with me</u> rather than <u>on me</u>. At any time after the first of the forty days following the meditation given below, you may feel free to attune to my vibration quickly. Simply focus on the third eye briefly and see me in your heart chakra taking only a few seconds and I will be with you. You will know what timing is best for you. Also you may invoke as many spiritual teachers as you please along with my vibration.

- Sit at your altar or in a place of solitude and quietness with your spine straight, even if sitting in a chair. If you can sit in the yogic posture, please do so, but it is necessary only that your spine be straight.

- Close your eyes and focus your physical eyes and attention on the Ajna chakra or third eye.
- Allow your mind to have any thought it wants to bring into your awareness and do not hold onto the thought. Simply allow thoughts to come and pass effortlessly out of your consciousness like a traveling cloud on a beautiful and quite summer's day.
- When your mind is stilled somewhat, gently move your awareness to the heart chakra and then focus your consciousness into the spiritual heart which lies in the vicinity of the physical heart.
- Know, feel or see a sphere of light in the spiritual heart and take your time to nurture the light through feeling your connection with my vibration.
- See me sitting in yogic posture in the middle of the light in your heart center. However you are aware of me is how it is for you and there is no right or wrong. I may appear to you as vibration, light, or physical form. Many of you will see my form as it has been presented to you through various picture reproductions from those whom I have chosen to come into contact with me in the Himalayas. It is all good.
- I now hand you a tulsi leaf, holy basil, which is not physical but simply a vibration of light which I use as a symbolic gesture of friendship now as we meditate together. Meditate with me for 10 minutes minimum and optimally one hour or longer each day for 40 consecutive days. If you choose, it would please me greatly if you meditate one hour or longer each of the forty days.
- I have projected Atma Kriya into your world in golden ray techniques of light through the teaching of Swami Vishwananda. Those of you who have taken the Atma Kriya Initiation and are practicing it may incorporate this time of meditation with me into your regular practice by using 10 minutes minimally of that time for this method. Those of you who have not taken the Kriya Initiation that Swami Vishwananda gifts mankind, I invite you at the end of the forty days of meditation with me to read

Appendices I and II of these epistles and determine if Atma Kriya is the path you wish to follow with me.

- I send my love to you eternally. I am at your service and await you at the time of your decision to sit with me in meditation ten minutes or one hour and more for forty successive days.

—Babaji

EPISTLE SEVEN

Utpalavati note to readers: Epistle Seven is addressed to Swami Vishwananda's disciples who also are disciples of Maha Avatar Babaji as well, some of whom are consciously aware, and some are not. Should you, the reader, not consider yourself one of those disciples, Babaji encourages you to read his *Epistle* as if you are standing within the Oneness Vibration of Babaji with his disciples and Swami Vishwananda. As I began to record the words Babaji was speaking, he handed me a euro coin that looked exactly the same as one Swami Vishwananda had given me in 2007 when I was visiting his Spiritual Center in Germany.

Babaji: To those who choose to listen to the sound of OM Within—the Reality of the Self,

When I gave you (Utpalavati) this coin through Swami Vishwananda, it stood as a commemoration of an initiation of Brahmacharis into his monastic order within the organization, Bhakti Marga. The evolution of Swami Vishwananda's work stands for his entry into the world of form as a leader of present-day young people who wish to dedicate their lives to God. In the early years, many who initially felt connected to their Guru, Swami Vishwananda and his organization, Bhakti Marga, fell by the wayside. The phenomenal daily life stresses of modern day enlivement of the ego processes of time, work, relationships and money issues took its toll as they applied to the success or failure of people to stay on the path of righteousness or dharma, right action.

We now stand together as brothers and sisters, in alignment with God, with fewer committed devotees as time and individual choices have decreased numbers. The monastic order that was within the organization of Bhakti Marga, has been dissolved by Sri

Swami Vishwananda as it has served its purpose in refining the birth process of those disciples who are committed to Swami Vishwananda, and to me, on that eternal spiritual path that leads to the Godhead wherein eventual Union With The Divine is assured. The organization of Bhakti Marga is contiguous but now without the monastic order orientation. Anyone is free to choose, for himself, both the monastic way of life and also simultaneously to live freely within Sri Swami Vishwananda's Bhakti Marga international community of spiritual attunement with The Divine.

Now is the time for those of you left standing as truly committed disciples of Swami Vishwananda to continue to build the trust and love alignment with the same focus you began. In the beginning you understood or comprehended the mission of your Satguru as your heart led you to align with his vibration. In times of trouble in life, where does the student of a Guru go to realign with the divine plan for his life? You all know that you go to the Divine Principle, God, whom the Guru divinely represents. It is to God that you pray and stay connected through the channels the Divine has given for your physical body, mind and essence to lead you back to the One.

It can rock your world when such an event as your Satguru or spiritual teacher dissolves the organization that nurtures your path takes place in the physical world. Ambition of those in the organization takes its toll in the process of purification of souls connected with such necessary structures as Bhakti Marga. *Understand also that not all Gurus and spiritual teachers have the mission to create organizations; and some do!* You all can see certain types of personality choices fall by the wayside as a structure is dismantled when its time comes. Trust the Satguru to know the proper time for *building or dissolving* such a structure and do not lament its demise. Like the phoenix that raises from the ashes to become a great light, so the ashes of Bhakti Marga's monastic order will bring forth Gruda, Vishnu's vahanna. Gruda comes in living color and transformation to alter what was yesterday into the beauty of tomorrow's tranquil blue and white purity of love divine. Let it be so for those of you who have chosen to stand with your teacher, Sri Swami Vishwananda, and walk forward with him into a new dawn of freedom's day.

Let us for a moment remember the times when Krishna walked your land and played the games that children play. He did indeed know the divine plan for his life expression from birth. Those about him questioned his divinity at those times when his behavior seemingly aligned more with the Earth vibration than the Divine. Yet throughout his Divine Incarnation, many aligned with Krishna and could not resist the Divine Love vibration that radiated from his being. Krishna's behavior was intentional so that Earth people at that time could align the heart and essence of themselves with the divine plan for Earth at that time.

In your time, history records the story of Krishna as Vedic scholars have sent it down through time to you. Likewise, future generations of planet Earth will tell the story of Sri Swami Vishwananda and marvel at the revelation of divinity reflected in his legacy to humanity of his time.

In present day, those of you left standing at the dissolving of the monastic order within the organization of Bhakti Marga are the committed disciples for whom Swami Vishwananda and I have been searching since his mission truly and officially began at the divinely predetermined age of twenty-seven in the Earth year 2005.

Now the reformation work begins in earnest. Stay firm in the Divine Love that rests in the heart of each of you for your spiritual teacher. Stay connected to the Divine Vibration of the Godhead and to me, Babaji. I stand here in your heart ever ready to lend a hand when you need me. Allow me to come to you in your meditations in the *Forty Day Meditation* I have designed for those of you who wish to spiritually progress through that method of attunement.

I am *Babaji,* one devoted to the progression of Earth incarnations into light, into freedom, into everlasting Love Divine. Attune your vibration to mine and you will know me, and you will know that you and I are One in Divine Love forever and ever.

—Babaji

EPISTLE EIGHT

Dear Friends who ring the bells of time,

When you, as a human being, incarnate into the density of Earth's environment, you are in full knowledge of the higher vibrations of light from where you have come, and why you are incarnating at that time. You stand in purity and with the true knowledge of your being, your soul. Soon, however, the birth process begins the long progression of forgetting man's true being that had been free to roam in the splendor of access to pure knowledge in the greater planes.

When you complete your allotted time in an incarnation, you as an individual soul leave the Earth Plane and return to soul origins. You then awake from the dream of your Earth incarnation and access your assets and liabilities from your recent life journey. From the ashes of your transition from the physical, your essence rises again into the Phoenix, once broken-hearted but now returned alive again into full glory. In these *Epistles* we wish to acquaint you again with the essence of your soul, the real being whom you knew so well when you entered the womb of your physical mother. We wish you to develop the ability to become enlightened while in the body, thereby becoming a Jivan Mukta. You are thus reborn into higher light essence of the greater planes of existence while embodied.

On the way to salvation or liberation of the soul, as many spiritual writings inform, you take many pathways along the life journey. You begin to grow in the toddler stage wherein you learn to walk by trial and error. Many times you bump your head, skin you knees and fall down only to courageously get up and try again and again until you toddle unsteadily around for some time. Eventually, you walk with grace and uprightness and you have learned to master gravity as it applies to the physical body and its equilibrium.

Later in life you will learn a different kind of balance when you learn to balance the physical form on the bicycle. Once you have learned to walk and ride a bicycle you have learned balance in a way that you never forget. Your very cellular nature remembers 'balance' and you no longer consciously need to think about how to walk or ride a bicycle. It has become as natural and automatic as breathing, or your heart remembering to automatically and rhythmically beat. Oh, my friends, I wish for you that you learn enlightenment and code it into your cellular nature even as you naturally have encoded 'balance' therein.

Soon after birth the white sands of time begin to take you to the inevitability of often great pain in relationships, work endeavors and exposure to the prestige, power and wealth areas so valued upon the Earth plane. Eventually you reach that place where you begin to ask *seriously* the questions of life that come to everyone: Who am I? Where did I come from? Where am I going? Those of you reading these *Epistles* may have been asking yourselves these questions for perhaps many years. We wish to assist you in answering these questions for yourselves from within the essence of each of you.

My friends, it is imminent and of the most importance that you meditate each day. You find enough time to do numerous activities throughout your day: bathing, grooming, dressing, cooking, eating, driving, working, shopping, a plethora of entertainments, reading, talking on the phone, texting on cell phones, using computers, sleeping and on and on. If you have the time to do all those things, why do you not have the time to meditate? From the essence of your true Self, you must cultivate a longing for Self-knowledge in the same way you acquire a desire for the other activities you perform each day.

Choose to transcend the almost paralyzing fear that arises when you get close to your true Self. The human ego is designed to help you cope with all the risks to the physical form that exist on Earth. The ego, along with your physical form, grows into monstrous proportions beginning from the time you are born and learn to walk until you ascend to the higher planes in transition and drop your body and it's ego. Your powerful ego fears you becoming enlightened and thereby the real you taking control of your life from the higher perspective while in the physical form. The ego is designed to be a helpmate, but presently humanity has made the ego his master. Through sincere meditation you can regain control over all your senses such as the yogis of the Himalayan mountains of India have attained and have given you the method through sacred scriptures such as the Vedas.

I wish to communicate to you what I know in absolute truth, you can become enlightened in the physical body while still residing in the world. You can relearn the sacred steps to enlightenment through sincere and purposefully dedicated meditation. Walk along with me by attuning to my vibration in the *Forty Day Meditation Technique* I have given you in *Epistle* Six. Thereafter learn *Atma Kriya* as taught and initiated by Swami Vishwananda. Learn to love yourself by attuning to the Divine Love in which you were created and projected into worldly existence. Walk in light, my friends, then gracefully and, *in balance,* you will bridge the New Golden Era just ahead on Earth's horizon. So let it be in the light and love of the Creative Force—God.

—Babaji

EPISTLE NINE

Dearly Beloveds:

Utpalavati: Jagatguru Maha Avatar Babaji appears in a vision standing in divine silvery-white light. His right hand and forearm then become focused in the light with his bodily form partially obscured as the light intensifies in vibrational attunement to the Divine Energy that he radiates and that pulsates with Cosmic Consciousness. In his hand Babaji holds a sphere of great light that dances and moves to the rhythms of His creative manifestation of light energy into the illusion of physical form. He gently and carefully closes his hand around the sphere of light as tenderly and lovingly as a mother holds her newly born infant and, with precision, casts the sphere into the world of form—Earth.

At this point Babaji instructs me to explain the nature of my visions. At times I perceive a scene in front of me in the room, and in most visions, I am aware of myself in two or more dimensions simultaneously. I am aware fully of my physical self sitting at my computer typing in the words I hear Babaji say. At the same time I am aware completely of myself in the dimension or vibrational levels in which I see and hear Babaji in the experiences I write, such as the one above.

Babaji: The Cosmic Lingam of life and death resides in my hand as light options merge with Cosmic Consciousness to bring into manifestation man's physical world. In Oneness with the Divine Mother, I hold the formula for life and death on planet Earth. I exercise, by Divine right, the ability to create human forms at will. My nature is Divine Love that wills itself into form. My purpose for being on planet Earth is to assist mankind into realizing the Self and eventual Union with the Divine—Oneness.

In time, each level of attunement to the Divine will manifest the knowing to carry the soul back to its origin. By the time the

Golden Era manifests itself completely into conscious awareness of the entire population on Earth, you will have recognized that the life you are living now, with all its struggles to reach higher light, has been the very vehicle, your Divine Vahana, which has manifested the Golden Age into your world. Embrace the troubles you create to carry you forward and transform them into light. Then, my friends, you will live upon your planet within Divine Awareness of the foretold prophecy of the Golden Era just beyond most of conscious knowing at this time.

Open the gate of the City Four Square*, my dearest friends, and walk through leaving behind the third dimensional energy of this life in the darkest days of the Kali Yuga Age in which you reside at present

I send you my love, along with the offer of assistance in the various ways I may choose to project Divine Energy into each individual consciousness. My friends follow me; I will lead you home.

—*Babaji*

*City

Four Square: Reference Maha Avatar Babaji's sacred yantra meaning of the square in Appendix III. And reference glossary.

EPISTLE TEN

Greetings,

Flowing throughout all your lives there has been a central theme or energy link that connects all that you have been and ever will be. That link of continuity is the essence or the soul that the Divine gifted when He "breathed the breath of life" into you. You have been and always will be divine energy given life from your Creator or Source. How then can you follow the current mind-set of collective consciousness on planet Earth back to your Source? It can not be, my friends. You must return your awareness to the point of birth, given life from the eternal light of forevermore— God.

Where is the knowledge you need to transport you back to your Source, your beginning without beginning and without end? Is it hidden in some great, secret spiritual book locked behind ancient monastery doors? Is it hiding behind an unseen door in Cosmic Consciousness? Is the knowledge you seek written by some famous saint long returned to higher realms? Does your local theater present the knowledge to you on the screen of moving pictures? Do you carry it within yourself and have forgotten how to access the knowledge you seek? Isn't knowledge of how to become God-realized, Union with The Divine, the knowledge you are seeking by reading these Epistles?

The Christ said in the *Holy Christian Bible*: "The kingdom of God is within. Seek ye first the kingdom of God and the rest shall be added unto you." Krishna said to Arjuna in the great Indian epic, *The Bhagavad Gita*, "Oh Arjuna, man looks for treasures outside in the world of form when the greatest treasure of all, living forever, resides within his own being."

Meditating With Krishna, The Lord Of The Universe

With Maha Avatar Babaji Guiding the Meditation

- Let yourself be free of external noise by sitting in a quiet place with spine straight.
- Light a candle unto the Great Lord of the Universe, Krishna, that one who brings delight to your soul likened unto that long ago time on Earth when he brought divine ecstasy to the gopies, the milk maids, of days gone by.
- If you have a picture of Lord Krishna and wish to place a flower offering there, please do so.
- In the Ajna energy center of the third eye see Lord Krishna sitting in the yogic position in a green valley with the magnificent snow-capped Himalayan sacred mountain range towering behind him.
- Perceive Mother Ganga rapidly flowing toward lower elevations at Krishna's side.
- Perceive the peace of Divine Light upon Krishna's countenance and request that He assist you to create that same peace in your own face and being.
- Perceive Krishna as he extends his hand and lovingly touches you at the anahata energy center, the heart area.
- Allow Krishna's Divine Unconditional Love to enter into your spiritual heart, trusting that you can receive what the Lord is offering you, His devotee, and His own.
- Meditate with Krishna for twenty minutes or an hour and we promise that you will know and feel the Cosmic Lord's love for you.
- Receive Lord Krishna's grace.
- I am with you.
- Know that Lord Krishna and you and I are one.
- Know we are one with all your heart, with all your mind and with all your soul.
- Feel the love of the Universal Lord of your being.
- Fly with Vishnu's vahanna, Guruda, into the wild blue yonder of freedom's gate.
- Know thyself and be free, my friends.
- Come home to freedom.
- Let peace descend upon your being.

I bless you. I bless you. I bless you. — *Babaji*

EPISTLE ELEVEN

Hello, I bid you salutations from the heart of Babaji:

In present day the planet's future existence is threatened with the weapons that were developed in the latter twentieth and early twenty-first centuries. In ancient times, before the wars of the present, man fought mainly face-to-face on the battlefields of history. The Lord himself, as Avatar Krishna, incarnated and used the war recorded in the *Mahabratha* to bring mankind the *Bhagavad Gita*, The Song of God. That Holy Scripture gives a formula for enlightenment and explains how mankind has the capacity to live in dharma, harmony and Love Divine. Krishna shows you in the *Gita* how to align your thoughts, words and actions with Divine Will for man.

In these Epistles I remind you of where you may find the formulas for enlightenment in past spiritual writings such as the *Bhagavad Gita* and the Christian *Holy Bible*. Many other Holy Scriptures that contain truth also exist from times past. Search out the ones that appeal to your inner being and read them as a refresher course so that your spirit may soar to the heights of Guruda, the Great Golden Eagle Vahanna of Lord Vishnu.

In conjunction with formulas for enlightenment given in past time, I acquaint you with the opportunity of *present day* formulas for enlightenment. I am offering you the opportunity to connect with my vibration in the *Forty Day Meditation* given in *Epistle Six*. That, too, is a formula for enlightenment should you choose to pursue with diligence your commitment to completion. And I provide information where you may locate teachings in the *Atma Kriya* techniques I have given to Swami Vishwananda (Reference Appendix I and Contact Information).

Many scriptures speak about the saints who have come to your planet to show you the way to *liberation*, giving their lives as an example. Swami Vishwananda and his disciples have begun writing a series of books telling the stories of certain saints from both east and west. It will please me if you, who read these *Epistles* will choose to search out Swami Vishwananda's work about saints. Study the examples of the varied lives of the saints and martyrs about whom Sri Swami Vishwananda has written and thereby attune to how saint have reached liberation while in the body, the Jivan Mukta. Use their examples as a blueprint for enlightenment. No! You do not have to become a martyr to become liberated. Reading about the saints provides another example of a formula for enlightenment.

In these ending days of the Kali Yuga Age the *easiest* way the Divine has given to reach enlightenment is the way Swami Vishwananda teaches: The path of devotion, Bhakti Marga. The primary spiritual practices he instructs his disciples to do are *Atma Kriya* (Reference Appendix I)*; Japa* (Chanting the names of the Divine using a japamala (prayer beads) or chanting continuously, silently within, as you go through your day; and the *OM Meditation* (Reference Appendix V). Also singing devotional songs (kirtan) and satsang (spiritual gatherings) are other spiritual attunements he encourages his devotees to practice . He teaches the ancient practices of Vedic fire yagnas and ritual worship of Divinity through murti pujas. I, personally, have given Swami Vishwananda the *Atma Kriya* techniques that form the foundation of his work on the planet in this incarnation—Opening Hearts to Divine Love. [See Appendix II]. *Again,* I recommend that you, who choose to align and connect with my vibration, seek out a course in *Atma Kriya* after you have completed the *Forty Day Meditation.*

I welcome you into the God-Self-Realized world of *Atma Kriya* when you have chosen to recognize that it is time to access Cosmic Consciousness. I welcome you home into the Eternal Light of the Divine Cosmic Father-Mother God!

—Babaji

EPISTLE TWELVE

Blessed Be, My Friends:

Utpalavati: Maha Avatar's Epistle Twelve dictation began with the experience of becoming aware that I am with Babaji in the Himalayas in light body. After a few minutes during meditation concentrating on the Ajna, third eye energy center, and at the point where a deep peace pervades my being, Babaji appears and I am with him early in the morning shortly before dawn. The Maha Avatar honors me with an invitation to pour the water for His early morning, ritual Ganges River bath. The youthful Babaji is sitting in a long silver tub dressed in a white, waist to knee-length dhoti. Maha Avatar's illuminated countenance looks toward the Ganges below and the towering snow-capped Himalayas in the distance. I stand behind him and pour several containers of Ganges water over His head; I feel blessed and humbled that he allows me to perform that sacred ritual.

When the Ganges water He has allocated for the ritual purpose is finished, Babaji stands up and turns to face me. Amazingly, beginning with His head and moving rapidly downward, the illusion of his physical body transforms into golden light even as His form is clearly visible. I see the Divine Babaji surrounded by luminescent golden light sending out radiant light beams in a sunburst design all around him; it is a most wondrous and beautiful sight. Babaji's pure radiant beauty of face and form is beyond description as it sends out brilliant, luminous, golden light in all directions around the sphere of Earth. The sun's bright dawn-breaking rays reflect off the Himalayan snow-capped mountains behind Babaji, seemingly born this very morning, destined to caress and illuminate the copper highlights in the Divine Babaji's beautiful, long dark hair.

My eyes are drawn to Babaji's heart area. A sphere of vibrating magnificent luminescent rainbow colors appear as spherical bands of color exactly in the order of a rainbow in Earth skies: red, orange, yellow, green, blue, indigo and violet. Each spherical rotation of the individual color bands transmits an audible sound vibration that resonates with the sound of creation—OM, OM, OM! I spontaneously know what Babaji is communicating as comprehension floods my consciousness. Babaji is Master of the five elements and the seven primary colors, the seven musical tones, all of it—the all of Earth design of the material world. He holds within his being the creative force that sustains Earth manifestation into material form through sound and light.

Maha Avatar says: "Follow me." Babaji leads me into a Himalayan cave just behind where we are standing. The cave is familiar to me as I have been here many times through countless millennia. He invites me to sit with him. Babaji says simply: "Write."

Babaji begins Epistle Twelve: Upon entry into physical form you carry with you the light body paralleling the one I have shown you through the eyes of my disciple during the Ganges bath ritual. The light body exists with me even as I present a physical body structure to those who see my light vibration appearing as solid form. The Divine creates a light body for the Himalayan masters who become liberated, even today, as they wander these mountain crags. It is also truth that every human from all time has the light body safely inside and around the physical form. Your light body is simply of a higher vibration than the material body.

The physical eyes do not have the capacity to see the spiritual or light body. When the body of light is seen, it is the third eye or spiritual eye that detects the vibration and sees it as light seemingly solidified. My dear friends, do become aware and let it pervade your consciousness that the physical eyes have limitations imposed upon you at birth. Attune yourselves to the Ajna energy center, third eye, if you would advance your knowledge of the higher vibrations of the etheric realms.

A physical visual example of how the third eye sees higher vibrations can be comprehended by using the electric fan of the material world. When the fan is not plugged into an electrical outlet or not switched on, your physical eyes clearly see the fan blades as solid mass. When the higher vibration of the fan, caused by electrical current speeding up the rotating movement of the blades is present, the physical eyes see through the blades. You do not see the individual fan blades but only a movement of light. Where do the blades go? Logic tells you that the blades are still there but your physical eyes do not perceive them but see only vibrating light. And so it is with the spiritual eye, it simply has the capacity by Divine Design to allow you to see the higher light vibrations. That is how the One taking my dictation sees me as both physical form and as light. Why do you not see the spiritual eye with your physical eyes? Logic informs you that first you must become conscious of the third eye, itself, and then you may see higher light vibrations that the third eye itself exemplifies.

My friends, truly it is time for you to perceive beyond the physical body and become aware that you are from birth a light body having a physical experience. Use the form as it is intended by the Divine Creator. Experience the world of Earth with the physical form but remember always that your true nature is light for eternity and forevermore. Relinquish fear of losing your identity without the physical body. Learn to remember that you are light and it is your birthright to remember this from within your essence, your soul light. *I have designed the Forty Day Meditation to give you the opportunity to realize the Self—the light body that you are now, always have been, and ever will be.* (Reference Epistle Six).

Oh, my beloved friends. come with me into light, into remembrance that you are Divine Eternal Light. I wish you remembrance. I wish you Divine Love. I wish you to become conscious of that which you always have been, Divinity ensconced in form so that you may experience Earth life in all its beauty and pain. Learn to remember that ecstasy and sorrow are the same when experienced with equanimity of mind and soul. Learn to conquer the Earth experience of physicality and you will see your own vibrating color wheel of creative energy within your heart.

That which I am, you are. I am ever available to you who attune to my vibration of light; I love you eternally. Come home to Light and welcome from One who has loved you always.

—Babaji

EPISTLE THIRTEEN

Greetings: From time immemorial I Am, even as you are, we are one:

Berries plucked and consumed from the vine bring nutrition to the body in a fresh content that packaged and marketed varieties do not have the capacity to contribute. The human design was intended to live more simply than it has been developed over the centuries. Now the population of the world knows that the balance of nature is virtually destroyed in Earth domains. Let you, my friends, begin to assist Spirit in bringing back the balance of nature on your world in the twenty-first century.

Look in your lives and begin to daily notice the things that are out of balance. Choose to find the courage within you to walk in the uprightness of peace, harmony, truth and love. There are countless straight-forward factors available wherein you may choose to help balance human use of nature's natural resources. For instance, you may choose to conserve energy in numerous ways. Do not waste! Let, *Waste not; want not; Om Namo Narayanaya,* become your mantra for conservation in the material world.

As a simple example of current extreme waste, think about the unspeakable amounts of waste in food thrown into the garbage heaps daily in restaurants around the world. It is a wasteful and diabolical way of using the large amounts of energy in the life-force of the natural food the Divine provides for mankind in Earth design.

Additionally, the energy of producing and preparing the wasted food is enormous. Add to this the energy of the people paying money accumulated from energy spent through their life-force in their work that subsequently purchases the wasted food. And it brings the total energy and resources of people and the Earth itself to a great cost in this one area alone. *Think about this and how it is only one way the life-force energy is misused on Earth in present day!*

My friends, resolve this moment to begin the process of being *present* to that which you do in all thought and action, and commit to bringing your life-force into alignment with Divine Will! Those of you who do the *Forty Day Meditation* and the *Atma Kriya* as taught by Swami Vishwananda, please use those times in connecting with my vibration to work with me in balancing these issues presently existing in your life. *I am available to anyone on Earth who is sincerely committed to evolving the soul into the higher vibrations of dharma, light and Divine Love.*

Have the courage to begin to live more simply. Notice if the lifestyle of the large cities of the world and your participation in it has made you happy and has resulted in you living a fulfilled life? Look at the faces around you; do adult faces reflect beauty, contentment and happiness? Look at the faces of some of those who are alleged to be the most successful in your world, those of the film industry. Look deeply into their eyes on the big screens you now view them upon and tell me, "Even with the artificial accoutrements of the trade that enhances physical beauty in the eyes of the world—Is the light of life brilliantly shinning from their eyes?" My friends wake up and take the first steps into balancing the life-force within you through the way you live in the material world and how you use the resources the Divine freely has given and provided for mankind.

Let the forces of so-called darkness recede into the void from whence they came through bringing light to your world in all of your thoughts and actions aligned with Divine Will. Have the courage to stand upright as God-man and live according to the tenets of old in alignment with the principles that bring about the balance of nature on your world. Begin to be a solution and vow to begin, by each thought and each action, to *not contribute* to the problem of the imbalance of nature in your material world.

Be courageous, be kind, be generous, be loving in all thoughts, words and actions. Let the times of your present world recede into the dark ages through your taking a stand to bring light into all thoughts and physical activities. Let go of the need to compete in the market place for prestige, success, name and fame. Let yourselves align with the Divine Will for inhabitants of planet Earth. Come home to the Creative Principle of Divine Love—and then live it—becoming a Jivan Mukta—a God-man. Come home now in your time to the Self-realized attunement to Divine Will.

—Babaji

EPISTLE FOURTEEN

Hello again, In the Divine Light of the One,

The time has come in humanity's future options to co-create with the Divine in producing the dharmic path to step upon that leads into the future of Earth production of human life. We travel along the highway of life in expectation that our wishes surely will be fulfilled completely through bringing our desires into material manifestation. Lo, my brothers and sisters of Light, I tell you this day in your time that the light which is seeded into your cellular natures as mankind must be aflame with truth. Take truth as your standard bearer if you care to carry into daily experience the seed crystals of the divine energy from which you sprung forth into life, and thereby fulfill your highest potential as humankind.

The door to eternity is open to you always. Let your every thought align with this knowing and bring your life and actions into Divine manifestation. Let this be brought forth from your potential as a seed thought within the Divine Mind of Eternity's flowing life energy. Let us stand for a moment on a precipice high in the Himalayas of India. Come with me in your meditative state of being and stand with me looking at the Sacred River Ganges 1,000 feet down in the valley floor. If the Divine told you to jump into the Holy Ganga below, are you ready to do so without hesitation? You must be ready at any time to detach from the physical body. That is the last bastion of surrender to the Divinity within you, for it is the physical body that detains you from reaching your goal of liberation into light body.

Run from the thoughts and actions that keep you bound in physical matter lifetime after lifetime. Choose now to read the *Mahabharata,* the *Bhagavad Gita* extraction especially. if you would learn as Arjuna did before you, to release attachment to the physical form. *My friends, I tell you this day that your time for hesitation is over.* Now the merging of the Kali Yuga into the age of Truth, the Sathya Yuga is at hand. You are within the energy of the Sathya Yuga as we stand together in your meditative state in truth and light on this precipice high in the Himalayas of India's holy ground.

Let me affirm for your edification that I have come into your awareness at this time in the preplanned totality of the Divine Plan. You, who are reading these simple *Epistles*, are those whom I have prepared through the ages and all of your lifetimes on Earth to be ready at this moment of your reading to come home to truth. What is the truth of which we are speaking? It is none other than the *truth of you*. "Know yourself and be free." You are an eternal being having a physical experience. For many of your lifetimes you have reversed that great truth, thinking instead that you are indeed a physical being having an Earth experience in the material world.

Let us continue with your meditations in the future. Do the *Atma Kriya* as taught by Swami Vishwananda and connect with me as I ever stand ready to lend a hand, an ear and my heart toward advancing you on your path into Living Truth. Walk with me in your future and together we will win the game of life on Earth. Come into truth of the Sathya Yuga and let us share the light with your fellowmen so that all may come into freedom of the soul to express love toward and with all life.

The animals are now ready to leap forward into higher consciousness even as you step forward in Divine Love for all life. Let us look at that possibility. You have been taught through Divine Scriptures of various spiritual teachings that a time was coming when the lion would lay down with the lamb, the elephant with the ant. Know that time is just around the corner of your awareness even as darkness seems to reign on Planet Earth at this time. It is "darkest before the dawn" do you remember?

Take my hand, follow your heart, and walk with me into your future of Light Body living on Earth in harmony and Love Divine. You are creating that Golden Era even in this darkest hour before the dawn, let me assure you. So take heart from the heart of

Babaji; I am ever with you and always will be. Come home to truth, the Maha Sathya Yuga, soon to fully manifest wholly and completely into your consciousness and your world. Amen and OM.

—Babaji

EPISTLE FIFTEEN

Utpalavati: In Meditation, I hear a voice say: "The Ancient of Days will speak with you." In the world of art, it has been said that "The Ancient of Days painting by William Blake vividly illustrates the conception of God as architect of the cosmos, the master builder who "set a compass upon the face of the deep."

The Ancient of Days Speaks in Conjunction With Jagadguru Maha Avatar Babaji—As One:

Peace be unto you:

From time immemorial man has taken the time for his daily prayers according to his beliefs that are aligned with his soul essence. Individual resonance toward a certain eternal spiritual path is programmed before incarnation and has been divinely and atmically designed to lead the soul back to The Divine. So it is that you, who presently are reading these *Epistles*, have been on the path which is recorded in your cellular nature from birth. It may seem to you that you have been struggling to find the time to pray or meditate as the needs of the physical body and the material world take all or most of your time; you so believe.

Please allow me to say to you this day that it is time for you to discard the belief that you do not have enough time to pray or meditate. Your entire life can be a meditation if you decide to make it so. Even work is worship, a prayer, a meditation if you dedicate it to The Divine. Those who enter your world as teachers sent from The Divine teach humanity to dedicate everything and all you think, say, or do to The Divine. In that way you will become in alignment or attunement with the Creator of The All.
Christ Consciousness is within everyone who is, has been or ever will be incarnated on Earth. The meaning of Christ Consciousness,

at its most basic comprehension, is as the Christ taught: "I and my father are one." (John 10: 30)

Additionally, in John 14: 12-14, Christ says: "Verily, verily, I say unto you, He that believeth on me, the works that I do shall he do also; and greater works than these shall he do; because I go unto my Father. And whatsoever ye shall ask in my name, that will I do, that the Father may be glorified in the Son. If ye shall ask any thing in my name, I will do it." That verse gives Christ's teaching and promise that all mankind can reach the Christ Consciousness that He exemplified. Christ Consciousness gives one the experience of the goal of life, which is to become surrendered and thereby unified with the Divine Will of Christ Consciousness, The Christ within all, Salvation—freedom. In Hindu spiritual tradition, Christ Consciousness is the same as Enlightenment in those terms. The Enlightenment of Krishna's teachings and the Salvation of Christ's teachings are _One and the same,_ but through _seemingly_ different spiritual paths or traditions.

Christ Consciousness Meditation

In the purest of intent, Divine Love and commitment to your enlightenment, We Three, being One in spirit—The Ancient of Days, The Master Christ and Maha Avatar Babaji, send forth into your vibrational fields and spiritual hearts the following meditation.

- Leave the struggles of materiality behind you as you *sit* for this meditation.
- When the connection with me [Babaji] has been made, look into the mirror of your soul for 10 minutes as you calm your mind.

- Look for the knowing, the visualization, the realization that you have been on the path of Christ Consciousness all your life. Look for divinity within you, no matter how you define it or by which religion or spiritual tradition that you have resonated with on your path seeking to reach The Divine.

Dear Friends,

In today's world, peace and tranquility can be difficult to find. Crystal Clarity Publishers and Clarity Sound & Light seek to support you in your efforts. Our products are created with one thought in mind — to help every individual find a sense of harmony within and with the world around them.

Many blessings to you,
The staff of Crystal Clarity Publishers

Name: _____

Address: _____

City: _____

State: _____ Zip: _____

Email: _____

Yes, I would like to receive:

☐ E-mail newsletter with articles, discounts and special offers. *Please supply email.*

☐ Information about Hot of the Press Book Club.

☐ Ananda Course in Self-Realization brochure.

☐ Program guide for The Expanding Light Retreat Center.

☐ Information about Ananda Church of Self-Realization.

Contact us:
800-424-1055
www.crystalclarity.com
clarity@crystalclarity.com

Crystal Clarity Publishers
14618 Tyler Foote Road
Nevada City, CA 95959

Stamp
Here

- Let your attention then follow your thought direction into the center of your spiritual heart in the vicinity of the physical heart. See, know or feel your spiritual nature within you.
- In love, peace and acceptance perceive an intense, luminous Christ Light therein.
- In the middle of the Light stands The Master Christ Jesus. He is dressed in a long, flowing white robe with the end brought forward from the fabric behind his left shoulder and draped across his left shoulder falling gracefully down the front. The Christ greets you with hand raised in blessing and a smile of pure love upon his countenance.
- The Christ looks directly into your human eyes and simultaneously into your spiritual eye. This also Sri Swami Vishwananda does when he blesses you in Divine darshan, cognitive of both your karma, which is truly maya, or illusion, and the divinity within you.
- Look into the mirror of yourself residing within the eyes of your Teacher, your friend, your brother, One in spirit with you—the Christ!
- The Christ reaches out his hand to you and therein is an etheric present.
- Let your soul recognize what The Christ is offering you. Surely Christ's gifts are individually given with Christ Consciousness and with Divine Love for each of you.
- As long as you choose to meditate, look into your own soul reflected in the eyes of the Great Master, The Christ.
- All that needs to be communicated at this stage of your soul evolvement, The Christ will seed into your brain pathways and into your spiritual heart. In days to come these seed crystals will burst open like the petals of a dewy, fresh, pure lotus blossom when the sun's rays lovingly caress its purity.
- Let it be your job to supply the light for Christ's gift to blossom within you in future days. The Christ knows what you require to move you forward on your spiritual path and is offering it to you as he stands in your spiritual heart—now!

The Ancient of Days, The Christ and Maha Avatar Babaji, being One in spirit, now say: We have given you thirteen steps in the *Christ Consciousness Meditation*, one representing each of the twelve disciples. The Thirteenth Step is the Christ standing in your spiritual heart ever ready for you to open the door—loving you and in peace forever blessing and guiding you throughout eternity.

The time for commitment to your path in a conscious way is given to you this day to bring the Light of the Heavenly etheric realm, itself, into awareness in your heart and soul. Know that this is so! Carry the message and the Love from your *Christ Consciousness Meditation* into your daily life, your daily prayers and meditations and into your every thought, word and deed. In that way you may become *enlightened* or *saved*, thereby realizing the truth of who you really are and, in greater truth, that which you always have been.

The Ancient of Days
The Master Christ
Jagatguru Maha Avatar Babaji
In Oneness
Bless you in the name of the
Most Holy Divine Principle—God.
Go In Peace and Divine Love.
Amen and OM

EPISTLE SIXTEEN

Utpalavati: Maha Avatar Babaji holds a Golden Apple the color of gold dust on the tips of His fingers that have been brought together forming a pedestal. Babaji holds the apple up close to His incredibly beautiful, celestial face while keeping His eyes focused on the apple. He sends the apple twirling around as it sits securely on the tips of his fingers. Babaji's ethereal, magnetic beauty, for a moment, seems to literally take the breath away! It feels as if we are in a null zone and that everything I know in the material world is no longer relevant. Time seems to stand still or is nonexistent. When the apple stops spinning, a small wooden drawbridge drops down and a tiny Babaji form dressed like a sentry sits down and slides down the bridge and stands at attention, saluting. I laugh in pure joy and wonder at the depth of Maha Avatar Babaji's love that has created a living Divine play, a living puppet show, for me to relate to you, his readers.

Babaji Begins Speaking:

Divine Beings:

Lo, from the dawn of time man has used his imagination as a pathway to freedom. The so-called imagination is within the mind and heart system of man given life from his first breath originating from the Source. Then let us use this imagination or will of man to further our knowledge, experience and love of the Divine Light Principle from whence we first came in our beginning—without beginning, without end. Your pure imagination, or will, has allowed you to perceive the vision of the Golden Apple I gave to the disciple who records these *Epistles* for you.

In present time, we go often from day-to-day in our lives as if on remote control. We begin our days and end our days in exactly the same ways. We act as if we are sleep-walking and our lives often become routine as we choose to live by rote. Meditation is a way for mankind to awaken the central core of his Being and, thereby, his life may become what it was meant to be in the beginning of beginnings.

Man may live with the capacity to be happy, to be free, and to be alive in the present moment without continually looking backward or forward in the present moment. In that way of being stands your life-force ability to weep in overwhelming sadness or feel and express great joy, both with the purest equanimity. Control of the mind is required to do this!

Babaji's Caution Pertaining to Judging Enlightened Masters

The Divine has sent to Earth Enlightened Masters from the realms of greater consciousness elevated in vibration beyond the vibratory level of the third dimension of this world. The Masters show you the way, a path to freedom through their life actions. *By their fruits, ye shall know them,* the Christ taught. And so it is!

Be ever vigilant when you decide to judge the words and actions of an Enlightened Master. Perhaps you do not yet remember that you eternally are enlightened but your purity is hidden by maya. If that is so for you, please remember that you do not have the knowledge of a Master's intent and his range of omniscient perception. Therefore your judgment must be purified by removal of the veil of illusion, maya, before you have the discernment to become fully aware of the truth of Enlightened Masters' words and actions.

The Masters have complete control of their minds and the five elements of Earth experience. That is the goal of each of you and of all mankind. Even a million lives on the wheel of karma sometimes transpire, through individual choice, for a soul to reach the stage of Self-God-realization. Why? As you may well know, it is the link to Earthly desires unfulfilled that draws the soul back again and again to Earth and the material form. And that is the

Earth experience so designed. You may take as long as you *will* to realize freedom. I am offering in these *Epistles* to assist those of you who are weary of the return of your soul to physicality over and over again through the wheel of incarnational cycles.

There is a Divine Plan for the current age and it is that the Kali Yuga and the Sathya Yuga exist together as the Kali Age now merges into the Sathya Age. Have you noticed that science has provided you with the opportunity to live in truth as technology and instant communication makes it more and more difficult to conceal anything one does or says? It is not a coincidence that in the Truth Age you are within the beginning stages even now, that your material world is converging with the spiritual world to bring forth the Divine Plan for truth to once again reign on Earth in both speech and actions.

The Divine has provided the easiest path to the truth of the Self in this age through meditation and calming the restless mind by chanting The Divine name with which you resonate. There are thousands. Even karma yoga (action]) is a form of meditation when it is dedicated to God! Do you understand that the name you chant is simply a verbal expression of the spiritual heart of each of you? When you feel love for that which you speak such as a Divine Name, it is the love from your own heart connected with the Oneness that will transport you into enlightened awareness. Meditation will assist you! *It is my purpose within these Epistles to provide a way for you to become committed to existing in Cosmic Consciousness for those of you who are prepared and ready.*

It is the way of a teacher to test the student; it is for the benefit of the student that the test is given as the teacher has already learned the lesson. The test is given so that the student knows where he stands with the lessons and if he has learned them or not. There are many divine opportunities encoded within the structure of the words in these Epistles. *One* of my tests for those of you who have read *this far* is in the form of *three* simple and energetic questions you may ask yourself. This test is not multiple choice but rather it is in a straight forward "yes" or "no" answer format.

Babaji's Three Questions For You

1. Will you commit to connecting with me in the *Forty Day Meditation* given in *Epistle Six?*

2. After completing the *Forty Day Meditation* will you seek out the work of Sri Swami Vishwananda's *Atma Kriya,* thereby determining if you sincerely wish to stay connected with me through the divinely inspired techniques? (Reference Appendix I).

3. Will you meditate daily using meditation as a pathway to freedom— Self-God-Realization?

Babaji's Interpretation of His Golden Apple Play (above)

In days gone by students gave apples to their teachers. Alas, in present day unhealthy fast food takes precedence.

*   The golden apple that you perceived in the beginning of this *Epistle*, in this case given from the teacher to the student, represents mankind's life possibilities as the Divine gives in wholeness, purity and perfection.
*   The twirling motion of the apple represents the wheel of karma man has created.
*   When the apple stopped spinning around represents these *Epistles* and Swami Vishwananda's *Atma Kriya* as your opportunities to get off the wheel of karma!
*   The opening that occurred in the form of a draw- bridge represents the opening of your spiritual heart to Divine Love.
*   The sentry (soldier, guard) who appeared, in truth, represents my vibration as the Cosmic Guide who has been with you always in all your incarnations.
*   My saluting you represents my form of greeting you within these *Epistles.*

- My sincere message in the *playfulness* of the Golden
  Apple Vision my disciple has recorded, and you have
  used your imagination to perceive is this: I reiterate what
  The Christ taught you: *Behold, I stand at the door and
  knock.* It is your choice to open the door and invite me in
  or not.

I love you one and all. From your beginning of beginnings I
have known you and loved you and I will love you into forever and
forever.

–Babaji

EPISTLE SEVENTEEN

Utpalavati: Swami Vishwananda, whose Guru is Jagadguru
Maha Avatar Babaji and with whom he is in perpetual Divine
communication, graciously and lovingly gave the following
meditation for inclusion in *Epistle Seventeen*. Babaji often refers to
Swami Vishwananda in his *Epistles*. He encourages you who read
them to search out the work of his Disciple, Swami Vishwananda
in *Atma Kriya*. More than once it has been emphasized that Maha
Avatar Babaji has given Swami Vishwananda the task of bringing
a higher vibratory level of *Atma Kriya* into present-day world
consciousness.

Sri Swami Vishwananda: The *Transmission Of Love
Meditation* opens the heart to greater love. Love is not meant only
to be accepted and kept, but love should be allowed to flow. When
love flows it is healthy. When one wants to imprison love it
becomes illness; that is what happens in this world. When love is
received many people keep it or use it to control others; that is
wrong. Love has to flow like a river. At the source of the river it
is small, but at the end when the river merges with the ocean, it is
large. The same is true with love that starts like a point in the
heart; when we let it flow it grows until it merges with the whole
which is GOD.

Jagadguru Maha Avatar Babaji: Swami Vishwananda has
given above a beautiful understanding that may encourage you to
incorporate his following *yogic technique* into your awareness and
yogic practice. The yogi does not practice only the higher
teachings while sitting in meditation; he faithfully incorporates
what he has learned into every thought, word and action. You
sometimes feel the intense vibration of love: for a newborn baby, a
lovely lotus flower, a golden sunrise, the love for your spiritual
teacher or Satguru—the intense feeling from your central being
that melts your heart. Adhere to the teaching of Sri Swami

Vishwananda and do not keep love when you feel it for yourself only. In awareness, send the love on a golden ray of light wave into your country and then around the sphere of Earth that hangs on nothing as your photographs from the American Space Vehicle clearly show you. Be aware that beyond the perception of your physical eyes and photographs, the Earth exists in the Divine Hands of the Eternal. Practice Swami Vishwananda's *yogic technique* of sending the love you feel all the way into Gods hands as Swami Vishwananda teaches you above and below.

Transmitting Love Meditation
by Sri Swami Vishwananda

- This meditation requires a partner—two people. Predetermine three things:
  (1) who will begin the meditation
  (2) the length of time you wish to meditate and
  (3) who will be responsible for keeping the time and signal when the time is complete
- Sit facing each other in the lotus position, with spine straight, eyes open.
- Look deeply into each other's eyes, the windows of the soul.
- Chant three OMs.
- The first person, predetermined, begins transmitting or sending love to the partner as you both continue to look, *with concentrated awareness*, into the eyes of each other.
- When the first person feels guided from within that he is complete, he will close his eyes briefly as a silent signal to his partner to begin transmitting *or returning the love vibration, (double, times two).*
- Continue alternating back and forth with each person taking a turn, paralleling the game of ping-pong, serve and return (double, times two) each time one serves or transmits.
- When the second person feels guided from within that he is complete, he briefly will close his eyes signaling that he is complete and his partner who began the transmission

will now transit love to the other person (double, times two) what he received.

- Continue for the predetermined time alternating between one person and the other, being present and conscious to doubling, times two, the transmission of the love energy you have just received each time you begin transmitting. When the signal is given that the allotted time has been reached, close your eyes for a few moments. *Feel the love as you have created it in your spiritual heart and send it outward to your country, the sphere of Earth and into infinity—the Hands of the Divine.* Chant three OMs together. With eyes closed, for a few moments, hold the Love Vibration close to your heart!

Note: Consider trusting that you are doubling (times two) the love vibration each time you are sending love through your spiritual heart's intent. In that way you need not be concerned about how to double the love you are sending each time. You may choose to be like the recent tennis shoe advertisement slogan: *Just Do It.*

Babaji: My dearest friends let it be!

EPISTLE EIGHTEEN

Utpalavati: December 24, 2008, Christmas Eve, I awoke in a state of bliss. I remembered being in the etheric with Maha Avatar Babaji, Swami Vishwananda and a group of people from Earth in our light body forms. I became aware that I had attended a satsang in the etheric while my physical form slept peacefully. I awoke ecstatically singing a beautiful song we had been chanting in the etheric dimension. Maha Avatar requested the inclusion of the experience in *Epistle Eighteen.*

We Are One
I am one with the stars.
I am one with the moon.
I am one with our Holy Divine Mother.
We are one ... we are one ... we are one.

I am one with the sun.
I am one with the cosmos.
I am one with our Cosmic Father.
We are one as man.
We are one as woman.
We are one, as love, in our heart of hearts.
We are one ... we are one ... we are one.

We are one with Christ Jesus.
We are one with the Buddha.
We are one with our Mother Divine.
We are one ... we are one ... we are one.

We are one with Sri Krishna.
We are one with the Great hero Ram
We are one with the Source of Creation.
We are one ... we are one ... we are one.
We are one ... we are one ... we are one.

Babaji: **Dear Beings from Celestial Stars:**

I come to you in the final Epistle of this series in the Divine Light of the Oneness we all are now and ever will be. Amen and Amen, OM.

A true Guru loves his disciple unconditionally. In present-day the Guru functions as a spiritual instrument much like a gyroscope. The Guru thus becomes the balancing vehicle between the disciple's present, or unenlightened state, and his true Divine state of being. When a Guru initiates you and accepts you as his disciple, he will inform in a most loving way that he has taken your karma. A Spiritual Teacher, such as Christ Jesus, lovingly will inform you that your sins are forgiven.

What does it mean in a literal or pragmatic sense when a Guru takes on the karma of his disciples? Christ provided the following example for future generations: (*Note--Utpalavati:* Babaji told the story in general terms and then requested that I quote it from the Bible itself). "And behold ,they brought to him a man sick of the palsy, lying in a bed: and Jesus seeing their faith said unto the sick of the palsy: *Son be of good cheer; thy sins be forgiven thee.* And behold, certain of the scribes said within themselves; This man blasphemeth. And Jesus knowing their thoughts said, "Wherefore think ye evil in your hearts? For whether is easier, to say, Thy sins be for-given thee; or to say, Arise, and walk? But that ye may know that the Son of man hath power on Earth to forgive sins, (then saith he to the sick of the palsy) Arise, take up thy bed, and go into thine own house". And he arose, and departed to his house. But when the multitudes saw it, they marveled, and glorified God, which had given such power unto men." King James Version of Holy Bible –Matthew Chapter 9:2-8

Babaji continues: In the Biblical story of the man with palsy, Christ, being an enlightened being with full power and so ordained from the Father, gives the example of the perfect Guru-disciple relationship through his interaction with the sick and paralyzed man. For the paralyzed man was sick unto death *from* his soul and had created in his physical body a so-called past karma was weighing so heavily on him in the present lifetime that he did not want to live and he was afraid to die. That same condition of fear of living and fear of dying exists in most of mankind today in your time. By choosing paralysis, the sick man stopped himself from material or worldly activities thus providing an avenue to contemplate how to find freedom from the wheel of karma.

When a child is sick with fever the mother lovingly takes no heed of all the time and trouble and will stay by the child's side until the sickness is alleviated and the child is physically well again. So it is with the Guru; he stays with his disciple through as many lifetimes as it takes to alleviate the fever, the sickness, the desire for material life, the wheel of karma.

Christ Jesus knew the past, present and future of the soul whose vibration existed within the physical form brought before him for healing. Like a mother who sits at the bedside of her sick child through the night until the fever breaks, Christ Jesus had stayed etherically with the sick man through his many incarnations. Jesus knew that it was the man's soul desire to transform himself into freedom from the wheel of karma, the return of his soul lifetime after lifetime to planet Earth. At the moment the paralyzed man looked into the eyes of Christ Jesus, his Guru of many lifetimes, from the depths of his soul he chose freedom. Christ knew this! He accepted the karma of his old disciple and therefore said: "Son, be of good cheer; thy sin [karma] be forgiven thee."

At the time of Christ's healing the paralyzed man many people knew that Jesus did not judge anyone. He acted out of love and true knowledge of past and present associations with the paralyzed man, his long-time disciple. The scribes' unbelief against Jesus was from ignorance. Christ knew this and forgave them instantly. And with love he taught those who would listen, those who '*had ears to hear*' the higher light of: *thy sins are forgiven* (or the Spiritual Teacher or Guru takes his disciple's karma).

Traditional Surrendering Body, Mind and Soul To The Guru Is Of The Past

The traditional model of surrendering body, mind and soul to the Guru or Spiritual Teacher is passé, obsolete. In present time the guru or spiritual teacher functions like a gyroscope, a balancing wheel. With his guidance you must do your *own* inner and outer transformation into enlightenment! The Divine Plan for surrender in today's time is to the Guru Within, your own Divine Self, God Within. You surrender or transform your ego into Divine Will with the true Guru or Spiritual Teacher's assistance, embodied and/or etheric.

When a Guru or Spiritual Teacher takes the karma of his disciple, most frequently the disciple does not instantly transform into an enlightened being. Frequently he still will have the life issues he had before: be it anger, jealously, greed, power, thirst for wealth, desire for name and fame or whatever life situations he has created. On occasion the person whose karma is removed by the Guru instantly is enlightened; in that case, it is by the Grace of God! When the karma (sin) that is hanging around the neck of the disciple like a heavy millstone is removed, the blessing or gyroscopic balancing of the Guru taking the karma opens a purified avenue *within the disciple.* The now clear pathway provides the opportunity whereby the disciple may more easily choose **not** to create any more karma through aligning with Divine Will rather than ego will.

It is the choice of the disciple what he will do with the gift of karma removed; truly the Guru or Spiritual Teacher has given a great Divine Blessing. How many of you have had this blessing? How many of you have squandered it and stayed in the morass of Earthly desires? *I know who you are.* I bless both those of you who have received the Guru's blessing of karma removal and *equally* those of you who have not.

Summation:

In these *Epistles*, I send you my blessings and offer you an opportunity to come home to freedom through my invitation for you to connect with my vibration both in *The Forty Day Meditation* and through Sri Swami Vishwananda's work with *Atma Kriya*. Please remember that is your choice if you accept these blessings or not.

My dear friends, we have come to *Epistle Eighteen,* the final in this series. In summary, I ask you: Have you heard the sound of rain on a tin roof? Hear the sound now from within, and remember me in the sound for we are one with the sound, the rain, the roof and the all. You are never alone. I am always with you even as all of creation is with you through your eternal connection with The Divine who gave you life through the soul, your essence. Like the millions of cells in the human body that comprise the one body, all of creation is One. And so it is!

Do you remember when you were young and your parents taught you lessons and you sometimes listened and sometimes you tuned them out? Do you remember when you were in school and your teacher sometimes gave you homework and most times you listened and did the homework and sometimes you did not choose to implement the teaching and do the homework? The same is true for those of you who finish reading all of these *Epistles.* For those of you who choose in the future to do the homework assignment I have given you by continuing to attune to my vibration in meditation, *I welcome you with all my heart!*

Know that those of you who have read thus far and *fully have opened your heart* and now *may* have tears in your eyes, *I know who you are.* Those of you, who have listened and subsequently will do your homework, be assured that *I know who you are.*

And remember that there is no right or wrong in any of this; it simply is!

As time as you know it meanders into your tomorrows, know that I am ever with you. Be at peace. I Am Babaji, One who loves you into forever and forever. Amen and OM.

AFTERWORD

by Utpalavati (Jean Peterson)

Included per Babaji's request

Maha Avatar Babaji explained in Epistle Two his purpose for including my experience in a certain meditation as an introduction to the *Epistle*: "The meditation offers a concise, coherent example of what is possible on the spiritual path as I work with my disciples in meditation through the millennia."

Paralleling the meditation in Epistle Two, Babaji instructed me to include the following experience with him in readiness to print this book after all his *Epistles* had been dictated and the cover and formatting of the book were complete. Babaji wishes to convey to his readers through this Appendix an *example* of the many and varied avenues of expression he may use when working with his readers. Maha Avatar Babaji has communicated that many who read His *Epistles* will choose to continue on their spiritual path by working with him through the *Atma Kriya* meditation work of Sri Swami Vishwananda. Babaji hereby informs his readers: "Please communicate to the readers that we do not wish to contribute to inflating the ego of anyone. Therefore, the spiritual experiences you share with readers, with my blessing to all, are offered in love and the wish to assist others as the primary purpose."

Maha Avatar's Blessing and Loving Teacher's Test:

As the experiences Babaji wishes me to relate unfolded, I was not aware consciously until near the end that they included one of his teacher-tests. You may recall that Maha Avatar spoke about such tests in Epistle Sixteen: "It is the way of a teacher to test the student; it is for the benefit of the student that the test is given; the teacher already has learned the lesson. The test is given so that the student knows where he stands with the lessons and if he has learned them or not."

The wondrous, beautiful, and blessed experience began in the etheric dimension while my physical form slept peacefully. Immediately on awakening from being in the etheric, Maha Avatar dictated a simple prose poem-message. After the poem was recorded, Babaji instructed me to interpret the meaning of the poem and then to write the entire experience with him in this appendix.

For over twenty years I have adopted as part of my sadhana (spiritual practice) the recording and interpreting of my experiences and dreams. This practice developed long ago in an attempt to learn and integrate into my life thoughts and actions the lessons my spiritual teachers conveyed. Since the mid-1980s, Babaji has been one of my spiritual teachers. In a sense, one might intuit that Maha Avatar Babaji has been training me all these long years to record and produce this book for him without my conscious awareness!

On the morning of February 5, 2009 I awoke from being in the etheric (a higher vibrational state than the dream state). One moment, I was with Maha Avatar Babaji and my Beloved Satguru Sri Swami Vishwananda in the etheric vibrational world and the next moment, I immediately awakened.

ETHERIC EXPERIENCE:

In a dimension of great light, I become aware of myself standing with Jagadguru Maha Avatar Babaji and my most beloved Satguru Sri Swami Vishwananda. Babaji stood in front of the space (it was not exactly a room as we know it) and Sri Swami Vishwananda was seated to his left. Swami Vishwananda was wearing a white silk robe, my favorite, like he sometimes wears when giving darshan on Earth.

Wondrous light filled the entire area. From among several people standing facing the two Guru forms, a man walked and stood in front of Babaji and spoke directly with him. He asked the question: "Am I spending too much time in meditation and not enough time in attending to my duties in the world? I did not hear Babaji's answer.

As the man stepped away I knelt in front of Babaji to speak with him as he remained standing. The crystalline light surrounding Maha Avatar suddenly intensified until it became brighter than the sun, but rather than golden, the light appeared to be silvery-white as moonlight can appear as it reflects light from the surface of a serene lake. I raised my right arm to shield my eyes and also to attempt to see Babaji as his form stood still faintly revealed in the midst of the luminous radiating light. I continued this for some time until I realized *that* I could speak with the light as Babaji was both the light and the form that he had presented earlier. The exact moment that *realization* dawned on me, I instantaneously awoke with no transition between the etheric and waking states.

In my now awakened state, Babaji distinctly said: "Write!" Can you imagine the power and sheer audacity of my ego after the just completed wondrous etheric experience, when I actually asked Babaji if I could write what he wanted later? My laptop had stopped working the day before and I planned to purchase a new one immediately. Since I knew for certain that Babaji, in essence, does not exist in time and space, my ego-thought was to record whatever Babaji wanted me to write on my soon-to-be newly purchased computer rather than writing it out in the slow longhand method. Maha Avatar readily and graciously agreed, but I clearly felt he was not greatly pleased with my ego-decision.

As Babaji's thoughts registered in my mind and heart, I aligned with his vibration as he had been teaching us in his *Epistles*. Through experiencing Babaji's inner counsel, I immediately *realized* my *huge mistake* and quickly asked Babaji to please excuse me. Immediately, I located pen and paper and recorded his following prose poem-message. Babaji requested that I interpret the poem in the way I have practiced my sadhana for many years as I explained above. Below you will find firstly the poem in its entirety. Then we have presented section by section along with the interpretation as I was guided to interpret it for inclusion herein at

Babaji's request. It provides an example for the readers of yet another way Babaji works with his disciples on their spiritual path.

BABAJI'S POEM

Sand trickles through the hourglass of time.
When time stops you know you have
Arrived in the Oneness of bliss.
Let bliss be . . . as it comes and goes.
Rest awhile in bliss when your toes know
What your head is doing.

Know with the totality of your essence
That the snows of winter melt into
Springtime flowers . . .
And India's Holy Ganges River
Flows into the greater oceans
Bringing Light and Unity into world view.

Let us join in the family of men and women
Walking into eternity's Light of forevermore.
Wear a smile of redemption*
As you learn to convey *Atma Kriya*
To all who seek it through sincere effort.

Thereby . . . Achievement of successfully
Walking with God is wrought!

redemption:
The liberation, enlightenment of Hindus and the salvation, deliverance, emancipation of Christians.

INTREPRETATION OF BABAJI'S POEM

I am certain that at least on one level, Babaji was testing my integration of his teachings while recording and producing this book of his *Epistles*. It has been my experience in the past with this type of sadhana that, in time, many levels may reveal themselves one-by-one.

Poem:
Sand trickles through the hourglass of time.

Interpretation: "Sand of time" represents life experience on Earth.

Poem:
When time stops you know you have
Arrived in the Oneness of bliss.

Interpretation: In the state of divine bliss, space and time (time defined as past, present and future) does not exist.

Poem:
Let bliss be . . . as it comes and goes.

Interpretation: Until one's enlightenment is achieved, bliss is experienced in time periods of minutes, hours or days rather than continuously. The Enlightened Masters, who incarnate to assist mankind on his path to enlightenment, exist in a continual sate of bliss hidden from the view of the eyes of the world while they simultaneously carry on their work in the world. The enlightened Masters, out of their great love for humanity come again and again to show the way.

Poem:
Rest awhile in bliss when your toes know
What your head is doing.

Interpretation: When one achieves the state of meditation wherein thoughts cease (the head) the toes of one's feet stop walking in the world due to no thought reaching the nerve pathways of awareness to create movement.

Poem:
Know with the totality of your essence
That the snows of winter melt into

Springtime flowers . . .

Interpretation: The winter snows represent the difficult times in one's life that merge into springtime flowers of the bliss of learned lessons that bring peace, fulfillment, harmony and divine love into life experience. Cycles of nature teach man as Maha Avatar teaches in *Epistle Five:* "Nature dawned on Earth and since that time, as you know it, nature began in all its sequential efforts to teach mankind the lessons of Divine Will. Nature has cycles from the rose in springtime bloom to winter's silence and then returning to spring and again the blooming."

Poem:
And India's Holy Ganges River
Flows into the greater oceans
Bringing Light and Unity into world view.

Interpretation: Out of the sacred Indian Himalayans where Babaji exists in his so-called Immortal Maha Avatar form, the pure mountain snows melt into the Holy Ganges River that flows into the greater oceans. This is a symbol of the teachings of the yogis of the Himalayas, including Babaji's teachings in these *Epistles* that, through the centuries, bring knowledge and wisdom (light) through the wisdom teachings flowing into the world-at-large, collective consciousness (unity).

Poem:
Let us join in the family of men and women
Walking into eternity's Light of forevermore.
Wear a smile of redemption*
As you learn to convey Atma Kriya
To all who seek it through sincere effort.

Interpretation: Maha Avatar Babaji and my Satguru Sri Swami Vishwananda have requested that I take the upcoming *Atma Kriya Teacher Training* Swami Vishwananda is offering at his center in Springen, Germany March 2009. Additionally, this section of the poem is given by Babaji as inspiration for readers, who sincerely seek knowledge of *Atma Kriya,* to consider working with Swami Vishwananda.

Poem:
Thereby, . . .
Achievement of successfully walking with God is wrought!

Interpretation: Jagadguru Maha Avatar Babaji's *Atma Kriya,* as taught by Sri Swami Vishwananda, when one sincerely practices in committed sadhana, has the power to bring Enlightenment— Unity With The Divine—hence Babaji's chosen title for this book, *Unity With The Divine.*

APPENDIX I

ATMA KRIYA

Atma Kriya is comprised of tools for transformation that reach all levels of existence: physical, energetic, intellectual emotional, mental and spiritual. It creates transformation that is a catalyst for reuniting limited human consciousness with the Atma, the soul, and thereby reuniting the Atma with Cosmic Consciousness. In essence, Atma Kriya is a powerful and potentially expeditious pathway to achieving Cosmic Consciousness – Unity With The Divine.

History:

Historically, Jagadguru Maha Avatar Babaji in the nineteenth century brought the ancient Kriya techniques and initiations back into world view and practice through his Indian disciple, Lahiri Mahasaya. Kriya practices as given to Lahiri Mahasaya continued to be taught in the early twentieth century by Sri Yukteswar Giri, Lahiri's disciple, as well as others. In 1920, Sri Yukteswar's disciple, Paramahamsa Yogananda, brought Kriya practices to the west in the United States and from there to the world-at-large. Presently, in the early twenty-first century, Maha Avatar has instructed Sri Swami Vishwananda to instill Atma Kriya into the world consciousness.

The Source of Atma Kriya:

Sri Swami Vishwananda was instructed by Jagadguru Maha Avatar Babaji to teach ancient Kriya techniques in 2007 then identified as Bhakti Kriya. Babaji informed Sri Swami Vishwananda in 2008 to change the identification of the Kriya techniques he teaches from Bhakti Kriya to Atma Kriya—Kriya for the atma or soul. Swami Vishwananda explains that currently the term Bhakti, meaning love and devotion, creates limitation in the minds of mankind that he *must overcome. True Bhakti transcends the mind.* However the atma, or soul, encompasses inclusive Cosmic Consciousness or awareness. Therefore for man's easier understanding and with Babaji's guidance, Swami Vishwananda changed the name of the Kriya he teaches from Bhakti Kriya to *Atma Kriya.* The World consciousness has evolved to the point that now humanity may comprehend that Atma Kriya techniques are divinely designed to assist the atma, the soul, to evolve into union with The Divine or enlightenment.

Originally the techniques in Atma Kriya were given by Maha Avatar Babaji to Lahiri Mahasaya. Since that time Babaji has contacted others of his embodied disciples, among them Swami Vishwananda and given them variations of the Kriya techniques. Additionally Swami Vishwananda includes both OM Healing and his own personally developed Trinity Meditation along with some variations of the ancient Kriya techniques into Atma Kriya.

APPENDIX II

My mission is to open the hearts of humanity to love by assisting
people to realize the divinity within them.
—Sri Swami Vishwananda

About Sri Swami Vishwananda:

From birth, Sri Swami Vishwananda has been living in the conscious presence of God. From the age of two he began to accompay his grandmother to the nearby Hindu temple where they performed daily worship. He visited churches and mosques as he felt drawn to The Divine in those sacred places. As a young boy he naturally began to meditate. From an early age he enjoyed spending his time singing devotional songs and performing spiritual worship. A natural spiritual teacher from birth, he inspired his childhood friends to participate in his inherent worship of the Lord. Sri Swami Vishwananda was born June 13, 1978 into a Hindu family on the island of Mauritius.

At the age of fourteen Swami Vishwananda experienced for the first time the state of *Samadhi,* a deep meditative state of absorption in the Divine. After completing his education, while remaining firmly grounded in the everyday reality of life, he began his life's work as a spiritual teacher traveling around the world.

In 2005 at the request of his *guru,* Maha Avatar Babaji, Swami Vishwananda founded a spiritual center in Germany that was relocated in 2008 and named Center Springen.

With natural ease Swami Vishwananda connects teachings from the Christian tradition with Hindu spirituality. He encourages us to deepen our own individual path to God and to continue any personal religion or beliefs. He embraces all religions and cultures. He teaches us to go beyond the concept of religion and to find the underlying unity, the unconditional universal Divine Love within. He respects and venerates all great masters, saints and sages from all religions and cultural backgrounds. Swami

Vishwananda asks us to love everyone in the same way and to see everybody as a part of God's creation.

Contact Sri Swami Vishwananda:
Website: www.bhaktimarga.org
Phone: +49 6124 727690

APPENDIX III

JAGADGURU MAHA AVATAR BABAJI'S YANTRA
The Meaning

Babaji's Yantra Depicted on Front Cover

Babaji's Yantra Overview: Maha Avatar Babaji's yantra is a graphic representation of his evolving mission to Earth. The yantra represents the Oneness Vibration of Love Divine that Maha Avatar Babaji exemplifies and teaches his disciples how to become. A long time ago Babaji gave his yantra diagram to the yogis in the sacred Himalayas. At that time the six points of the star did not touch the sides of the square. Likewise the four sides of the square did not touch the circle.

Babaji's explanation of his yantra as given for this book, *Unity With The Divine* incorporates changes he has made since his original yantra was given to the yogis of the Himalayas. *Babaji:* "At the time the yantra was given to the yogis, mankind was at a certain vibratory level whereby his understanding was that he was separate from the Godhead and the rest of creation. In present time, the understanding of the Oneness of creation and that everything is linked thereby is commonly known. Humanity as a whole is in the awareness vibration that many people seriously are beginning to incorporate the Oneness vibratory field into their energy fields and daily lives, their very essence. My yantra as I have given it for the purposes of this book, *Unity With The Divine*, reflects mankind's current awareness level by joining the symbols that comprise the yantra into One contiguous unit—the Oneness vibratory field." Reference the Yantra diagram on the previous page and the book front cover.

Definition of the word, yantra: A yantra is a symbolic geometric spiritualized design usually pertaining to a particular deity; ritual diagrammatic representation.

SYMBOLS:

Large outward Circle: Represents Cosmic Awareness; all that is, The Divine—God. The circle depicts the unlimited nature of creation without beginning or end. Babaji has come to assist humanity in perceiving beyond his limitations through striving for Cosmic Consciousness or Enlightenment, the unlimited. His yantra is a visual explanation of his mission and his purpose for being on planet Earth.

Square: The square is equivalent to the point beyond Earth's density where Cosmic Awareness meets Earth's density. The four Vedas are represented in the square as Maha Avatar is Master of the Vedas. All the Vedic knowledge and wisdom resides in Babaji, without limit.

Six Pointed Star: The star consists of two sacred geometric triangles. The *downward pointing triangle* represents humanity's divine opportunity to merge with Cosmic Consciousness through the descent of The Divine Avatar to Earth's density—Jagadguru Maha Avatar Babaji. The *upward pointing triangle* represents the inherent divine gift of humanity's ability to strive to reach Cosmic Consciousness—Enlightenment, Self-realization, God.

Sphere in middle of Six-pointed Star: The circle represents The Divine Heart from which everything originates and flows outward to the Star, the Square and the Circle of Cosmic Awareness, All That Is—God.

APPENDIX IV

FORTY DAY MEDITATION RECORDING CHART

Day	Date	Amount of Time In Meditation
Day One		
Day Two		
Day Three		
Day Four		
Day Five		
Day Six		
Day Seven		
Day Eight		
Day Nine		
Day Ten		
Day Eleven		
Day Twelve		
Day Thirteen		
Day Fourteen		
Day Fifteen		
Day Sixteen		
Day Seventeen		
Day Eighteen		
Day Nineteen		
Day Twenty		
Day Twenty One		
Day Twenty Two		
Day Twenty Three		
Day Twenty Four		
Day Twenty Five		
Day Twenty Six		
Day Twenty Seven		
Day Twenty Eight		
Day Twenty Nine		
Day Thirty		
Day Thirty One		
Day Thirty Two		

__Day Thirty Three__ _____

__Day Thirty Four__ _____

__Day Thirty Five__ _____

__Day Thirty Six__ _____

__Day Thirty Seven__ _____

__Day Thirty Eight__ _____

__Day Thirty Nine__ _____

__Day Forty__ _____

__NOTES:_____

_____

_____

_____

_____

_____

_____

_____

_____

_____

_____

_____

_____

_____

_____

_____

_____

_____

_____

_____

_____

_____

_____

_____

_____

_____

_____

Contact Information

JAGADGURU MAHAVATAR BABAJI
Contact in Meditation - *Reference Epistle Six*

SRI SWAMI VISHWANANDA
Germany
Center Springen
Email: registration@bhaktimarga.org
Telephone: +49 (0) 6124=72769-0
        (Tues – Sat 09:30 – 13:00 and 14:00 – 17:00)

ATMA KRIYA YOGA INSTITUTE
Am Geisburg 4
65321 Heidenrod-Springen
GERMANY
Email: info@atmakriya.org

UTPALAVATI (Jean Peterson)
www.KriyaOmPress.com
Email: Utpalavati@bhaktimarga.org
Office: +011 303 841 0928

GLOSSARY

AHIMSA—non-violence; to avoid causing harm to any living being consciously and deliberately by cultivating the knowing that one supreme dwells in all beings.

ANCIENT OF DAYS—The Divine Principle, God.

AJNA CHAKRA—One of the main seven energy centers located alone the spine in the human form. The Ajni Chakra is located between the eyebrows and also is known as the third eye chakra.

ARJUNA—Hero of the war depicted in the *Bhagavad Gita* whose charioteer was Lord Krishna.

ATMA—Soul; the inner motivating force in everything; universal assimilation and perpetual movement; eternal Divine Principal.

ATMA KRIYA—A powerful and expeditious path whereby one may achieve Unity With The Divine or Enlightenment. Atma means soul; Kri means action and Ya means awareness or Unity With The Divine through performing every action with awareness from the soul, the essence of the Self.

AVATAR—Incarnation of God; descent; Divinity descends to the human level teaching humanity how to become Divine.

BABA—Father.

BABAJI, JAGADGURU MAHA AVATAR—Immortal and Divine Being lovingly working for millennia to assist evolving humanity into Unity With The Divine.

BHAGAVAD GITA—Song of God; teaching song of Lord Krishna; the essence of the *Upanishads,* excerpted from the *Mahabharata,* the Indian spiritual epic.

BHAKTI MARGA *and*
BHAKTI MARGA MONASTIC ORDER—*used in this book as the*—Monastic Order established by Sri Swami Vishwananda that was founded in 2005 and dissolved in 2008. Bhakti means love and devotion; marga means path—bhakti marga is the spiritual path of love and devotion. Swami Vishwananda retains a spiritual center in Springen, Germany with an organization named Bhakti Marga without monastic orientation.

BRAHMACHARI—A monk who lives a life of self-discipline and sense-control, and meditation while remaining celibate.

CHAKRA—One of seven main energy centers along the spine in the human physical form.

CHRIST CONSCIOUSNESS — Also it is known as Cosmic Consciousness — Oneness; awareness that all of creation is connected or linked as one energy or spirit that originates from the One Divine Principle -- God. A state of being where one exemplifies Christ's qualities and teachings that symbolize the potentiality of what human nature can become. To achieve Christ Consciousness one must look within and bring the knowledge and wisdom forward into action emulating Christ as the example of ' "the way the truth and the life."

CHRIST JESUS—See Jesus Christ.

CITY FOUR SQUARE—City described in the *Bible* in the book of *Revelation.*

COLLECTIVE CONSCIOUSNESS -- Also mass mind—The state of mankind at present where all minds of man are connected or linked.

COSMIC LORD—Divine Being with awareness of the cosmos, all of Creation.

CRUCIFIXION—A form of execution used in ancient times that involved binding or nailing the victim to an upright cross until death; *used in this book* as the agony and death of Jesus Christ on the cross at Calvary.

DARSHAN—Sight of a holy person; bliss of the vision and blessing of the Lord.

DHARMA—Right action; the eternal principles of right action (righteousness) that are the foundation or Divine Cosmic Laws of creation.

DHUNI—A sacred fire; the dhuni often is kept burning continually in a ritually-constructed pit and is usually attended by a saint or a dedicated person.

DIVINE PRINCIPLE—God.

DIVINE, THE—The spirit or essence within all of creation originating from the same Source—The Divine Principle, God.

DISCIPLE—A student of a Spiritual Teacher or Guru.

EGO—Sense of the individual self, as distinct from the outside world and other selves.

EINSTEIN, ALBERT—German-born American physicist and Nobel laureate, best known as the creator of the special and general theories of relativity and for his bold hypothesis concerning the particle nature of light. He is perhaps the most well-known scientist of the 20th century.

ENLIGHTENMENT—Realizing the true Self; awareness of the Self as Divine, connected in Oneness with all of creation.

EPISTLE—Letter, missive, dispatch.

ETERNITY—Time without end, infinity.

ETHERIC—Greater vibration or dimension beyond Earth.

GANDHI, MAHATMA—Indian Guru; nationalist leader, who established his country's freedom from English rule through a nonviolent revolution (ahimsa).

GANESHA—The elephant-headed Hindu God who is said to possess the attribute of remover of obstacles.

GANGES— Holy, sacred River in India, used interchangeably with Ganga.

GANGA, MOTHER—The Divine Mother in the form of the Ganges River in India.

GOD—The Divine Principle, The Supreme, The Creator.

GOD-REALIZED—One whose consciousness has reached the realization that God and he are one; unity with The Divine.

GOLDEN AGE [Golden Era]—The next age after the present age of Kali Yuga, age of darkness; also known as the Sathya Yuga or age of truth.

GURU—one who dispels the darkness of ignorance; a spiritual guide

GURUDA—Vahana or vehicle of the Hindu God, Vishnu.

HEART CHAKRA—One of the seven main energy centers along the spine of the human form. The heart chakra is located alone the spine at the location of the physical heart.

HIMALAYAN MOUNTAINS—Sacred mountain range of perpetual snows in India where many yogis live, and through experience have produced the sacred Hindu scriptures, the Vedas. The immortal Jagadguru Maha Avatar Babaji has resided there for millennia in the same and different forms.

HINDUISM—A major religion and religious tradition of South Asia, the oldest worldwide religion, characterized by a belief in reincarnation and a large pantheon of gods and goddesses who represent aspects of the One God or Divine Principle.

HITLER, ADOLPH—The German political, military leader and one of the 20th century's most powerful dictators. Hitler converted Germany into a fully militarized society and launched World War II. Hitler hoped to conquer the whole world.

HOLY SCIENCE, THE—Book written by Sri Yukteswar as requested by Jagadguru Maha Avatar Babaji. The book demonstrates, by explanation of parallel passages from the Hindu and Christian scriptures, the essential unity of the great religious teachings of East and West.

INCARNATION—Embodied in a physical form. In religion, the assumption of an earthly form by a God.

JAPA—repetition of a mantra

JAPAMALA—prayer beads used for reciting repetitions of prayers or mantras [chants]. The japamala facilitates focus during meditation and spiritual practices.

JESUS, CHRIST—The Christ of Christianity, born in Bethlehem in Judea. In Christianity, the crucifixion of Jesus is believed to save the individual from eternal punishment through Christ's death on the cross.

JIVAN MUKTA—Self-God-Realized while in body.
JOHN, DISCIPLE OF CHRIST—One of the twelve, primary disciples of Master Christ Jesus; the disciple whose prophetic vision provides the content of the book of *Revelation* in the *Christian Holy Bible.*

KALI YUGA—Present iron age; age of darkness at present merging into the next age known as The Golden Age or time of Sathya Yuga—the age of truth.

KARMA—action; activity undertaken with desire; the fact of every activity having its inevitable consequences and of human destiny being shaped by the accumulative effect of all these consequences.

KARMA, WHEEL OF—Repetitive return of the individual soul to incarnations on Earth due to the result of desires unfulfilled.

KRISHNA, LORD—Avatar Krishna, The Divine Cosmic Lord; incarnation of Vishnu; teacher of the *Bhagavad Gita;* he who attracts, draws the mind toward him; pure essence; the Supreme Principle.

KUMBHA MELA—A spiritual gathering held in four Indian cities three years apart, once in each city every twelve years. Seekers come to spend time with saints and spiritual leaders, teachers, gurus.

LAVA— *In this book—* the name of the disciple Maha Avatar Babaji writes about in Epistle Five. Also one of the twin sons born to the Great Ram of India and his consort, Sita.

LIBERATION—Self-Realized God consciousness; freedom that once attained, frees mankind from the wheel of karma resulting in repetitive incarnations in physical form.

LIGHT BODY—Greater vibratory body comprised of light that is the soul or spirit of mankind.

LINGAM—An oval-shaped object representing the cosmic egg of creation; the creative energy of The Divine; God.

LORD OF THE UNIVERSE: References one of the Gods such as Krishna, Vishnu, Brahma, Shiva.

MAHA—Great.

MAHA AVATAR—a great avatar; physical manifestation of The Divine on Earth.

MAHABHARATA—the great Indian epic from which Lord Krishna's venerated *Bhagavad Gita* was extracted.

MAHASHAYA, LAHIRI—Disciple of Jagadguru Maha Avatar Babaji who lived in India. Babaji reinstated the ancient teaching of Kriya Yoga into the twentieth century through the teaching and Kriya Yoga initiations of Lahiri Mahasaya.

MANTRA—A sacred sound, chant or prayer.

MANDELA, NELSON—After his imprisonment of 27 years convicted of: "sabotage as well as other crimes" committed while he led the movement against apartheid. Subsequently, Nelson Mandela won the Nobel Peace Price in 1993.

MAYA—The force through which the infinite is experienced as being finite; illusion.

MEDITATION—Stilling the mind; technique of focusing the mind, based in part on Hindu meditation. Meditators may be given a *mantra* (a word or phrase) to repeat over and over in the mind.

MONASTIC ORDER—Life as practiced by persons who have relinquished the world for spiritual reasons and devote their lives, either separately or in community, in pure spiritual perfection. Vows of celibacy, poverty, and obedience usually are taken.

MUDRA—A symbolic hand or finger gesture producing a specific desired quality imparted to the person practicing the mudra. Mudras are commonly used and depicted in Christian, Buddhist and Hindu iconography.

MURTI—A statue used in puja or ritual worship in which a deity is (the ocean of milk) for a millennium seeking the divine nectar of the gods, amrita. Finally the gods obtained the amrita.

OCEAN OF MILK—The place where the gods and demons worked together for a millennium churning the sea to extract the nectar of the gods, amrita, thought to bestow immortality. Eventually the gods acquired the amrita.

OM—The Divine sound of creation; primal sound principle.

PLANES, GREATER—The dimensions in the etheric or greater vibratory levels beyond Earth.

PRANA—The life-force or breath.

PUJA—Worship; ritual worship in which a deity is invoked in an idol (murti) or picture.

RAM, AVATAR—Avatar of India; central figure of the Indian epic, *Ramayana,* story of Ram; an incarnation of Lord Vishnu.

RELIGION: A fundamental set of beliefs and practices generally agreed upon by a group of people. These set of beliefs concern the cause, nature, and purpose of the universe, and involve devotional and ritual observances. They also often contain a moral code governing the conduct of human affairs.

REINCARNATION—Born over and over into physical form; wheel of karma.

REVELATION, BOOK OF—Book in the Christian *Holy Bible* wherein the disciple of Christ Jesus, John, reveals his prophetic vision.

SADHANA—Spiritual practice.

SALVATION—In Christianity, individuals are thought of as being saved from eternal punishment through Christ's death on the cross.

SAMADHI—Spiritual absorption; the eight rung of raja yoga. Word used to define a yogi's conscious exit from his physical body.

SATGURU—The true teacher; divine master who guides the disciple all the way to God—enlightenment, truth.
SADHANA—Spiritual practice, spiritual quest.

SATHYA—Truth.

SATHYA YUGA—The next age; age of truth, age following the present Kali Yuga, age of darkness.

SATSANG—A Sanskrit word combining "Sathya" meaning "truth" and "sangha" meaning "group"; Gathering of spiritual people for meditation, prayer, devotional singing, chanting, keeping good company, fellowship; often refers to a meeting with a Guru or spiritual mentor.

SELF-REALIZED—The goal of spiritual seekers to reach the consciousness of Self-God-realization—Oneness or unity with The Divine Principle—God.

SHIVA—One of the Hindu Trinity of Gods: Brahma, Shiva, Vishnu. Shiva's abode is Mount Kalis in India and he is worshiped as the Destroyer-Regenerator God of the Hindu Trinity.

SIDDHI—A power or accomplishment that may be achieved through yogic practices that usually accompanies inner development; siddhis are sometimes present at birth
SPIRITUAL HEART—Located near the physical heart; home of the soul essence of the individual.

SRI YANTRA—A symbolic diagram of the human structure and the cosmos both manifested and unmanifested.

SUSHUMA—The central channel of the spine leading to the highest states of consciousness.

SWAMI—A spiritual teacher, Master; one who has renounced worldly activities in order to dedicate his life to God.

THIRD EYE—See Ajni Chakra.

TULSI LEAF—A leaf of the tulsi or basil plant considered sacred in Hinduism; the favorite leaf of Vishnu—God as the sustainer, protector.

YOGANANDA, PARMAHANSA—Indian Guru; Disciple of Swami Sri Yukteswar Giri of India. Yogananda is author of the venerated *Autobiography of a Yogi* and founder of the USA spiritual center, Self Realization Fellowship.

UTPALAVATI [Jean Peterson]—Disciple of Jagadguru Maha Avatar Babaji. Person whom Babaji requested to record his mind-to-mind and heart-to-heart dictation that is recorded in this book.

VAHANA—Vehicle.

VEDAS—The source book of revealed wisdom experienced by the great sages in deep meditation.

VEDIC SCHOLARS—Those who study and teach the Vedas; sacred writings of knowledge and wisdom by sages received through experience and deep meditation.

VISHNU, LORD—One of the Hindu Trinity of Godhead; Vishnu, the Preserver, Sustainer of the Vedic Trinity.

VISHWANANDA, SWAMI—Of Indian descent, born on the island of Mauritius, Africa in 1978. Disciple of Jagadguru Maha Avatar Babaji. Center Springen in Germany is Swami Vishwananda's international spiritual center. Swami Vishwananda teaches Atma Kriya at the request of his Guru, Maha Avatar Babaji.

VOICE OF GOD: Usually references the "voice within" each individual soul essence, the God Within.

YOGI--One who practices yoga, union with The Divine; yogi position or posture sitting with spine straight and legs crossed on thighs.

YUKTESWAR, SRI—Indian Guru; Disciple of Lahari Mahasaya; author of the book Maha Avatar Babaji asked him to write, *The Holy Science;* Guru of Parmahansa Yogananda.

ABOUT UTPALAVATI
(JEAN PETERSON)

Utpalavati, *Jean Peterson,* was born in the eastern part of the United States of America in the state of West Virginia. She is a writer, poet and publisher. Jean owned a small publishing company, Meridian Light Publishing in the 1990s. Jean's present publishing company, Kriya Om Press, was created to distribute her current book *Unity With The Divine* by Maha Avatar Babaji. Jean was married and has three children, one daughter and two sons. She lives in the Rocky Mountains of Colorado in the United States of America.

From birth Jean has been aware and conscious of the Divine inheritance with which each person is born. That Divine Right encompasses the potential to personally know and to be aware and consciously linked with the Creative Divine Principle, God. From birth Jean has been blessed with some of the siddhis as identified in both Christianity and Hinduism. The "gifts of the spirit" of Christianity and "siddhis," the yogic powers of Hinduism, potentially may arise for everyone during the spiritual journey and sometimes are present at birth. Throughout her lifetime, any monetary gain received through the utilization of these spiritual gifts Jean has used for further spiritual work or donated to charity. Among Jean's spiritual gifts is her remembered ability to be consciously connected with many of the Spiritual Masters from past Earth history. Her conscious connection with the Master Christ Jesus was instrumental in the writing of her first book in 1990, *Oneness Remembered.*

Jean's next book containing her spiritual memoirs and entitled *Rama's Bridge* is scheduled to be released in the spring of 2010.

You may contact Utpalavati (Jean Peterson):
www.kriyaompress.org;
Email: utpalavati@bhaktimarga.org; jean@kriyaompress.org
Phone: +011 303 841 0928